California Travel Guide 2024

Everything you need to know, When to go, what to see, and what to do in California's vibrant destinations - Your 2024 travel

Bobby L. Knowles

Copyright Page

Table of contents

Introduction to California

Enter the colorful tapestry of California, where every scene and city has a story to tell and every moment is an adventure just waiting to be discovered. As a passionate traveler and explorer, I have explored every inch of this incredible state, taking in its breathtaking scenery, varied cultures, and endless opportunities for adventure. I am now overcome with nostalgia as I write these words, thinking back on all of the numerous events and memories that have influenced my trip through California.

It all started with my first step onto Santa Monica Beach's sun-kissed sands, where the briny wind greeted me warmly and whispered dreams of limitless opportunities. After that, I meandered through the busy streets of Los Angeles, where aspirations and dreams pulsate through the city. Stars are born and legends are made in Hollywood, and I was mesmerized by its allure among the city's recognizable palm trees and glistening skyscrapers.

Beyond its glitzy exterior, California is a state of contradictions and contrasts, where vast deserts envelop the viewer and untamed beaches meet rocky mountains. In one instant, I was hiking through Muir Woods' majestic redwoods and marveling at nature's towering giants; in the next, I was navigating Big Sur's winding roads, each curve revealing an even more breathtaking view than the one before.

I did, however, really come to understand California's essence during those peaceful times when I was removed from the bustle of the city. Every experience I had, whether it was enjoying a farm-to-table dinner in the lush fields of Napa

Valley or standing on the Mendocino cliffs and watching the sunset, will always have a special place in my heart.

When I think back on my trip through California, I am reminded of the innumerable people who came before me and who each contributed a unique piece to the state's rich fabric. And now, as I extend an invitation to you to set out on your journey across the Golden State, I implore you to live fully in the present, relish each encounter, and allow California to enchant you.

So, dear reader, I invite you to journey with me through the heart and soul of California, whether you're planning a first-time visit or coming back to revisit old haunts. When you explore the wonders of the Golden State, let these pages serve as your inspiration, guide, and traveling companion. Because in California, the experiences are lifelong and the journey never ends.

Greetings from California. Greetings on this once-in-a-lifetime journey.

• Welcome to California

Welcome to the Golden State, where each sunrise holds the possibility of a brand-new journey and each sunset creates breathtaking views of the sky.

You're about to set out on an adventure through the heart and soul of California—a state known for its breathtaking scenery, extensive history, and seemingly endless possibilities—as you grasp this travel guide. I give you a warm welcome and an invitation to explore the magic that is waiting for you in every corner of this amazing state, whether you are an experienced traveler or a first-time visitor.

You'll find a wealth of advice, suggestions, and insider knowledge in these pages to help you get the most out of your visit to California. Discover the hidden treasures and recognizable sites that make California genuinely unique with each chapter, which takes you from the sun-kissed beaches of Southern California to the majestic peaks of the Sierra Nevada.

However, this guide is more than just a compendium of useful knowledge; it is a monument to the spirit of exploration that permeates every traveler's veins upon entering California. It's an ode to the variety of experiences, cultures, and environments that make this state a miniature version of the entire globe.

So, whether your dreams involve hiking among the towering redwoods of Yosemite National Park, exploring the energetic streets of San Francisco, or taking a wine-tasting tour through Sonoma County vineyards, know that you're in for an incredible experience that will leave you with lifelong memories.

Let yourself be enthralled by California's boundless possibilities, moved by its splendor, and inspired by its rich past as you turn the pages of this book. California beckons you to write your chapter in its illustrious history, whether you're looking for adventure, relaxation, or just some quiet time to yourself.

Thus, my dear traveler, keep in mind that the voyage itself is the destination as you embark on this enormous adventure. Savor each second, treasure every encounter, and allow California's enchantment to lead you on an unparalleled exploration journey.

The Golden State is yours to explore. Greetings from California.

About This Guide

Greetings and salutations from your indispensable traveling companion for California—the best travel guide ever created to make your trip even more enjoyable.

The goal of this guide is to be your go-to source for complete information, insider knowledge, and suggestions so you can travel through California with ease and confidence. Whether you're organizing a long road trip, a family holiday, or a weekend escape, this guide will help you make the most of your time in California.

Scope: This guide covers every corner of California, making sure that no place is left unexplored, from the sun-kissed beaches of San Diego to the majestic peaks of the Sierra Nevada. You'll find everything you need to organize and carry out your California adventure, including thorough chapters on historical background, useful information, dining and cuisine, nightlife, top attractions, day trips and excursions, technology, museums and galleries, and more.

Qualities:

Professional Advice: Take advantage of the firsthand knowledge and experience of an experienced tourist who has explored the many cultures and landscapes of California.

Insider Tip: Discover off-the-beaten-path attractions, hidden gems, and insider knowledge that will enhance your vacation and leave you with genuinely unforgettable memories.

Useful Tips: Get helpful guidance on travel, lodging, weather, safety, and other topics to guarantee a hassle-free and easy trip from beginning to end.

Cultural Highlights: Get a deeper understanding and appreciation of the distinctive identity of the Golden State by immersing yourself in California's rich history, lively culture, and diverse culinary scene.

Arrangement: Every chapter has been carefully arranged to offer a smooth reading experience and quick access to the data you require. This guide has everything you need, neatly laid out, whether you're looking for ideas for your next trip or useful tips for organizing your schedule.

Call to Action: Step out confidently and curiously on your California adventure. Let this guide serve as your compass and road map as you venture out into the wide world of opportunities that lie ahead of you. California extends a warm welcome to all visitors, be they a family looking for adventure, a couple on a romantic retreat, or a single person looking to make lifelong memories.

• How to Use This Book

Here is your all-inclusive travel guide to California! Here's a rundown of how to use this book and navigate it to make the most of your trip through the Golden State:

1. Introduction: To become acquainted with the goal and scope of this guide, start by reading the introduction. The introduction's storytelling will inspire you as you embark on your Californian adventure.

2. Table of Contents: This table of contents serves as a guide to the information within this book. Each chapter has been thoughtfully arranged to give you the knowledge you need to organize and carry out your adventure in California.

3. Historical Background: Learn about California's rich past, including the arrival of the Spanish, the gold rush, and native inhabitants. Learn more about the cultural legacy that has shaped the identity of the state.

4. Useful Information: Get helpful tips on a range of topics, including how to get to California, how to get around the state in a car, how to book lodging, how to read the weather, and how to travel safely.

5. Dining and Cuisine: Discover the wide range of culinary options available in California, including farm-to-table restaurants, regional specialties, and must-try eateries. Learn about the tastes that characterize California.

6. Entertainment and Nightlife: Take in California's thriving entertainment and nightlife scene, which includes rooftop bars, live music venues, theaters, and cultural festivals. Discover the ideal method to relax and take in the nighttime culture of the area.

7. Top Attractions: Learn about the must-see sights and recognizable landmarks that have made California well-known throughout the world. There is something for everyone to explore, from Yosemite National Park to Disneyland and the Golden Gate Bridge.

8. Day Trips and Excursions: Arrange amazing day trips and excursions to discover the hidden treasures and varied landscapes of California. This chapter is full of ideas, whether your interests are in hiking, wine tasting, or touring historic sites.

9. Technology and Innovation: Learn about California's status as a center for technological innovation, from virtual reality attractions and tech museums to Silicon Valley startups. Find out what the newest technological trends are influencing.

10. Museums and Galleries: Discover the thriving arts and culture scene in California, which includes historical sites, science centers, and world-class art museums. Learn about the legends and inventiveness that characterize the cultural legacy of the state.

11. Beyond the Guidebook: Conclude your travels with insider advice on how to experience California like a native.

To get the most out of your trip, find out about opportunities for community engagement, sustainable travel practices, and hidden gems.

12. Index: Throughout the book, use the index to quickly locate particular details or interesting subjects. The index will make it easy for you to find any attraction, restaurant, or helpful tip you're looking for.

Let this guide be your reliable travel companion and inspiration as you set out on your journey through California. California beckons you with open arms to make lifelong memories, whether you're looking for adventure, relaxation, or cultural immersion.

Chapter 2. Historical Background

• The Indigenous Peoples of California

A rich tapestry of indigenous cultures and communities flourished long before weEuropean explorers and settlers arrived in California, nestled within its breathtaking landscapes. For thousands of years, these indigenous peoples lived in harmony with the land, from the untamed Pacific coasts to the lush valleys and majestic mountains. This chapter delves into the rich and varied cultures of California's indigenous peoples, examining their past, present, and future.

1. Overview of Indigenous Traditions: Learn about the various indigenous groups and tribes that call California home; each has its language, traditions, and customs. Discover the profound relationship that exists between indigenous peoples and the land, as demonstrated by their cultural ceremonies, subsistence methods, and spiritual beliefs.

2. History Before Columbus: Discover California's pre-Columbian past, which dates back thousands of years to the time when the state's first indigenous peoples arrived.
Explore the advanced societies and civilizations that arose, such as the Ohlone, Chumash, Miwok, Pomo, and numerous others, all of whom left behind exquisite works of art, intricate architectural designs, and rich oral traditions.

3. Cultural Practices and Traditions: Learn about the diverse cultural practices and customs of the indigenous peoples of California, such as ceremonial dances, storytelling, basket

weaving, and pottery making. Learn about the cosmologies and spiritual beliefs that shaped indigenous communities' interactions with the natural world and the universe.

4. Impact of European Contact: Examine the profound effects of European contact on the indigenous peoples of California, including the loss of ancestral lands, the destruction caused by violence and disease, and the suppression of their culture. Discover the tenacity and defiance of native American tribes against colonialism, as they struggled to protect their culture and claim their right to self-governance.

5. Current Concerns and Rejuvenation Initiatives: Examine the issues that California's indigenous peoples are currently facing, such as land rights, environmental preservation, and cultural revitalization. Learn about the remarkable initiatives taken by indigenous communities to preserve their cultural legacy for coming generations by reclaiming their heritage, language, and customs.

6. Heritage Centers and Cultural Sites: Explore historical sites and cultural centers devoted to conserving and honoring the heritage of Native Americans across the state of California. Discover the significance of locations like the Kule Loklo Coastal Miwok Village, the Chumash Painted Cave State Historic Park, and the California Indian Museum and Cultural Center.

Consider the lasting impact that the indigenous peoples of California have left behind and the significance of respecting and maintaining their traditional legacy. Seize the chance to gain knowledge from indigenous viewpoints and voices to promote mutual respect, understanding, and cross-cultural cooperation.

Take a moment to recognize and pay tribute to the indigenous peoples who have lived in California for thousands of years as you explore the state. Their legacies, tenacity, and stories keep enhancing California's cultural fabric and beckoning us to embrace a closer bond with the land and one another.

• Spanish Colonization and Mission Era

Take a trip back in time to the Spanish colonial era, a significant period in California's history that influenced the state's cultural landscape and left a lasting legacy. We explore the reasons behind Spanish exploration, the founding of missions, and the long-lasting impact of this era on California's identity in this chapter.

The first step in the history of Spanish exploration in California is to trace it back to the expeditions of Juan Rodríguez Cabrillo and Sebastián Vizcaíno, as well as the arrival of Gaspar de Portolà and Junípero Serra. Examine the Spanish ambition to conquer the New World and extend the Spanish Empire through religious conversion, wealth, and power.

2. Creation of the California Missions: Discover the history of the California Missions, a network of missionary settlements founded by Franciscan friars to convert native Americans to Christianity and secure Spanish rule over the area. Explore the mission's architectural and cultural legacy, which is typified by its adobe buildings, bell towers, and vast grounds.

3. Life in the Missions: Learn about the day-to-day activities of those who live in the missions, such as Franciscan friars, Spanish colonists, and Native Americans who have converted to Christianity. Examine the various aspects of mission life that influenced the economy, society, and religion: from crafts and agriculture to religious rituals and cultural absorption.

4.The impact of the missions on indigenous peoples should be examined, taking into account the forced labor, cultural suppression, and disease that wiped out indigenous populations. Discover the tenacity and fortitude of native American groups against colonialism, as they overcame the difficulties of integration and worked to protect their heritage.

5. Legacy and Heritage Preservation: Consider the Spanish missions' enduring impact on California, ranging from their influence on architecture to their part in forming the state's distinct cultural identity. Examine the restoration projects, educational initiatives, and interpretive programs that are being undertaken to preserve and protect the missions as significant historical and cultural landmarks.

6. Controversies and Reckoning: Address the issues raised by the missions, such as disagreements about how they treated native Americans, the effects of colonization on the variety of cultures found in California, and the need to make sense of this complicated legacy.

Talk about how Spanish colonization has affected indigenous communities to this day and how it has affected California's collective memory and identity more broadly.

Consider the long-lasting effects of the mission era and Spanish colonization on California's history, culture, and identity.

Think about how crucial it is to face this complicated legacy in the context of a larger discussion about justice, healing, and cultural preservation.

While you investigate the ruins of California's mission history, pause to consider the tales of tenacity, adjustment, and cross-cultural interaction that have shaped the Golden State. Through a deeper appreciation of the many cultures and peoples that call California home, we can be inspired by this important chapter in the state's history.

• California Gold Rush

Travel back in time to the turbulent California Gold Rush era, a pivotal time in the Golden State's history that permanently changed its economy, culture, and landscape. This chapter takes us on a voyage of exploration and revelation as we follow the beginnings of the Gold Rush, its effects on California and the country, and its lasting legacy.

1. Origins of the Gold Rush: Learn about the circumstances that led to the 1848 gold discovery at Sutter's Mill, including the attraction of California's Wild West, the promise of wealth, and the allure of Manifest Destiny. Discover the critical role that James W. Marshall played in setting off a wave of speculation and excitement that quickly swept the country after his accidental discovery of gold in the American River.

2. The California Gold Rush: See the explosive influx of intrepid travelers and fortune seekers from all over the globe as word of California's gold spread like wildfire. Learn about the difficulties and struggles that miners encountered traveling westward in pursuit of wealth, enduring hazardous routes, severe weather, and uncertain futures.

3. Boomtowns and Mining Camps: Learn about the vibrant, practically overnight, boomtowns and wild mining camps that changed the face of California and its people.
Discover the vibrant multiculturalism of these frontier communities, home to immigrants pursuing the American Dream from China, Europe, Latin America, and beyond.

4. Economic and Social Impact: Look at the significant effects of the Gold Rush on the economy and society in California and the United States, including the emergence of racial tensions, the rapid development of cities and industries, and the eviction of indigenous peoples. Think about how the Gold Rush continued to influence California's reputation as the "Golden State," signifying the quest for prosperity as well as the promise of opportunity.

5. Women and Minorities in the Gold Rush: Bring attention to the frequently untold tales of women and minorities who were laborers, activists, and business owners who were vital to the Gold Rush. Examine the roles that Native Americans, African Americans, Latinos, and other marginalized groups played in the growth and prosperity of California's mining sector.

6. Environmental Impact and Legacy: Address the ways that the Gold Rush left an environmental legacy that continues to influence California's natural resources and landscape, such as pollution, habitat destruction, and deforestation.
Think about the continuous efforts to lessen the effects of mining on the environment and protect California's wild areas' ecological integrity for future generations.

Consider the lasting effects of the California Gold Rush and how important it was in determining the course of the state's development. Think about the lessons that can be drawn from this pivotal time in California history, such as the value of social justice, environmental conservation, and cultural preservation.

Let's pause to pay tribute to the pioneering spirit, tenacity, and resolve of those who came before you during the California Gold Rush. We can better appreciate the diverse range of experiences that make up the Golden State if we comprehend and welcome this important period in California history.

- ## Rise of Hollywood and the Entertainment Industry

Take a trip through the glittering world of Hollywood and the entertainment business, where legends are brought to life on screen, dreams are realized, and stars are born. This chapter delves into the beginnings of Hollywood, its quick ascent to international renown, and its ongoing influence on popular culture and the arts.

1. Hollywood's humble beginnings: Learn about the early days of Hollywood as a remote outpost tucked away in the hills of Los Angeles, far from the thriving city it would eventually grow to be. Discover the fortunate combination of elements, such as Hollywood's sunny weather, varied scenery, and proximity to important transportation hubs, that led to the city becoming the center of the entertainment industry.

2. The Birth of the Studio System: See how this unmatched center of creativity and invention was created by bringing together brilliant performers, aspirational businesspeople, and visionary filmmakers to form the studio system. Examine the ascent of renowned film studios like Paramount, Warner Bros., MGM, and Universal, each of which shaped Hollywood's terrain and left a lasting legacy in the history of film.

3. The Hollywood Golden Age: Enter the glitzy realm of Hollywood's greatest creative and cultural period, which gave rise to enduring masterpieces and recognizable stars.

Admire the lavish movie palaces, lavish premieres, and legendary figures that characterized this heyday of film, enthralling viewers with their romantic, exciting, and mysterious stories.

4. Hollywood Icons and Legends: Honor the enduring celebrities and legendary directors who contributed to defining Hollywood's heyday, from screen queens like Audrey Hepburn and Marilyn Monroe to cinematic visionaries like Alfred Hitchcock and Orson Welles. Discover the enduring legacy of the biggest stars in Hollywood, whose works still inspire and amuse audiences today.

5. Technological Advancements and Industry Significant Events: Observe how the introduction of sound and color, as well as the development of computer-generated imagery and digital effects, transformed the film industry and the art of filmmaking.
Learn about the influence of iconic movies like "Citizen Kane," "Gone with the Wind," and "Star Wars," which redefined the genre and pushed the bounds of storytelling.

6. Hollywood Today and Tomorrow: Consider how Hollywood has changed in the digital era as social media, streaming services, and globalization have altered the entertainment scene. Think about the opportunities and difficulties the entertainment sector faces in the twenty-first century, from the emergence of new content formats and distribution models to issues of diversity and representation.
Think back to Hollywood's lasting influence on popular culture, the arts, and society as a whole. Think about the

lessons Hollywood's ascent to fame has taught us about the value of creativity, teamwork, and tenacity in the pursuit of artistic excellence.

Take a moment to admire the artistry, inventiveness, and sheer magic that have made Hollywood the global center of entertainment as you explore its glitz and glamour. We can appreciate Hollywood's rich history and the stories, characters, and experiences that enthrall audiences worldwide more fully if we are aware of it.

Modern Developments and Cultural Influences

Enter the vibrant, ever-changing world of contemporary California, where diversity, innovation, and creativity come together to form the character of the Golden State. This chapter delves into the contemporary advancements and cultural factors that have catapulted California to the forefront of international movements and trends.

1. Technological Innovation: Explore the dynamic ecosystem of technological innovation that characterizes California, from the tech behemoths of Silicon Valley to the thriving startup scene in places like Los Angeles and San Francisco. Discover the ground-breaking developments that are transforming industries and promoting economic growth in areas like biotechnology, artificial intelligence, renewable energy, and space exploration.

2. Urbanization and Infrastructure: Take note of how quickly California's largest cities are growing, with skyscrapers, busy neighborhoods, and cutting-edge infrastructure changing the state's urban environment. Discover bold endeavors like renewable energy programs, high-speed rail, and sustainable urban planning projects that seek to solve the problems of population increase, climate change, and transportation in the twenty-first century.

3. Cultural Diversity and Fusion: Honor the diverse range of cultures that make up California, where individuals from all origins, lifestyles, and ethnic groups coexist to form a thriving

and welcoming community. Discover how cultures collide and merge to create distinctively Californian expressions of creativity and identity through the fusion of cultural influences in music, art, fashion, and cuisine.

4. Sustainability and Environmental Preservation: Examine California's stance on environmental sustainability and conservation more closely. The state has taken steps to combat climate change, support renewable energy, and preserve natural habitats. Learn how government policies, environmental organizations, and grassroots movements have shaped California's standing as a global leader in environmental conservation and stewardship.

5. Social Justice and Activism: Examine the history of social justice and activism in California, encompassing the fights for racial justice, gender equality, and immigrant rights as well as the civil rights movement and LGBTQ+ rights. Discover the powerful voices and movements promoting inclusion, equality, and social change at the local, national, and international levels that have arisen from California's diverse communities.

6. Global Influence and Soft Power: Consider California's role as a major player in politics, the tech sector, and the entertainment industry. Its exports of culture have shaped attitudes and trends globally. Think about California's influence on international dialogue and how innovation, sustainability, and social advancement will develop in an increasingly interconnected world. Consider the contemporary advancements and cultural impacts that have molded

California's identity, ranging from urbanization and technological innovation to cultural diversity and environmental preservation. Think about the opportunities and difficulties California faces in the twenty-first century, as well as the part that people, groups, and organizations will play in determining the fate of the Golden State.

Take a moment to observe how innovation, diversity, and creativity interact dynamically to define the identity of the Golden State as you explore the state's modern landscape. Understanding and embracing these contemporary advancements and cultural influences will help us steer California and beyond toward a more promising, inclusive, and sustainable future.

Chapter 3. Practical Information

• Getting to California

With confidence and ease, set out on your journey to California, the state of dreams and limitless opportunities. This chapter contains all the necessary details and advice to make sure your trip to California is stress-free and runs smoothly from beginning to end.

1. Transportation Options: Examine your options for getting to California, including flying, taking the train, taking the bus, and driving your vehicle. Discover the principal bus, train, and airport terminals that service California's major cities and regions. Weigh the advantages and disadvantages of each mode of transportation.

2. Air Travel: With so many domestic and international airports servicing cities like Los Angeles, San Francisco, San Diego, and Sacramento, take advantage of the ease and accessibility of traveling to California by air.
When organizing your air travel to California, research the major airlines, flight paths, and airport hubs. You should also take into account aspects like cost, convenience, and travel duration.

3. Train Services: Take into account the picturesque and relaxed alternative of visiting California by train. Amtrak provides routes like the California Zephyr, Coast Starlight, and Pacific Surfliner that link important cities and areas. Discover the facilities and services offered by Amtrak trains,

such as cozy seating, delicious food options, and stunning views of California's varied landscapes.

4. Bus Lines: Greyhound, Megabus, and other bus companies offer routes that connect major cities and regions throughout the state. Consider the flexibility and affordability of traveling to California by bus. Find out about bus terminals, timetables, and ticketing options. If you're traveling short distances or on a tight budget, think about how convenient taking the bus can be.

5. Driving Routes: Driving routes like the Pacific Coast Highway, Route 66, and the Sierra Nevada Scenic Byway offer amazing views and unforgettable experiences. When considering travel to California by car, think about the freedom and flexibility that comes with it. Make sure your car is ready for long-distance driving and plan your itinerary, making sure to include stops at famous sites, national parks, and hidden treasures.

6. Travel Planning Advice and Tips: Learn useful guidance and pointers for organizing your trip to California, such as looking into available modes of transportation, purchasing tickets ahead of time, and taking the weather, traffic, and travel restrictions into account.

Look through online travel guides, travel apps, and discussion boards to get the most recent information and advice from other travelers. If you want more specialized help, speak with a travel agent.

Think back to the thrill and expectation you felt when traveling to California, as well as all the adventures you have in store for the Golden State. Take into account the travel experience in its entirety, including the logistics of getting to California, and seize the chances for exploration, discovery, and connection that arise at every turn.

Let this chapter's advice and information serve as a roadmap as you get ready to travel to California, guaranteeing a smooth and pleasurable trip from the moment you arrive in the Golden State. California welcomes you with open arms and invites you to start the journey of a lifetime, regardless of how you choose to get here—by plane, train, bus, or automobile.

• Transportation Within the State

Once you're in California, the journey never ends as you take in all that the state's famous landmarks, dynamic cities, and varied landscapes have to offer. This chapter contains all the information and advice you need to know to make the most of California's transportation system and make the trip from big cities to isolated wilderness areas easy and enjoyable.

1. Public Transportation: Learn about the accessibility and convenience of the buses, light rail, subways, and commuter trains that are offered in California's major cities.
Discover routes, schedules, and fare options for various transit systems, including the Los Angeles Metro, the San Diego Trolley, and the Bay Area Rapid Transit (BART) in the San Francisco Bay Area.

2. Ride-sharing and Taxi Services: Take into account how handy ride-sharing services like Uber and Lyft are for navigating cities and reaching locations that are difficult to get to by public transit. When selecting a mode of transportation, take availability, cost, and convenience into consideration. You can also learn about the taxi services that are offered in popular cities and tourist locations.

3. Rental Cars: Take advantage of the flexibility and freedom that come with renting a car to see California's vast landscapes and outlying locations, such as national parks, picturesque drives, and rural areas. When choosing a rental car, research the companies, policies, and insurance options available. You

should also take into account things like size, fuel economy, and road conditions.

4. Cycling and Walking: Take advantage of this healthy and environmentally beneficial way to see California's urban areas, coastlines, and picturesque paths. Examine bike-sharing programs offered in cities like Los Angeles, San Francisco, and San Diego, and stroll through pedestrian-friendly zones filled with eateries, retail establishments, and cultural sites.

5. Inter-City and Regional Transportation: Use inter-city transportation options like buses, trains, and shuttles to plan your trips between California's cities and regions.
Examine local bus services provided by Greyhound and Megabus, as well as long-distance bus services provided by the Pacific Surfliner, Capitol Corridor, and San Joaquin trains.

6. Travel Planning Advice and Tips: Learn useful guidance and pointers for traveling throughout California by investigating available options, making travel plans, and buying tickets ahead of time.
When making travel plans, take into account variables like traffic, weather, and local events. You can also look for the most recent information and suggestions by using resources like websites, maps, and transit apps.
Consider the variety, practicality, and chances for adventure, exploration, and discovery that come with California's transportation options.
Think of the logistics of getting around the state as an integral part of your overall travel experience, and welcome the

voyage as a chance to fully immerse yourself in California's communities, culture, and landscapes.

Allow the details and advice in this chapter to serve as your roadmap for traveling throughout California's transportation system, guaranteeing a smooth and pleasurable experience as you take in the attractions of the Golden State. Open roads, picturesque routes, and countless opportunities for exploration await you in California, whether you choose to travel by bicycle, public transportation, or rental car.

• Accommodation Options

Finding the ideal spot to relax and rejuvenate before you set out on your journey through California is crucial to a pleasurable and comfortable experience. This chapter examines the wide variety of lodging choices found across the Golden State, ranging from opulent resorts and boutique hotels to quaint bed & breakfasts and reasonably priced hostels.

1. Hotels and Resorts: Take advantage of the comfort and elegance that come with lodging in California's largest cities, seaside resort areas, and resort areas. Examine the facilities offered, including restaurants, fitness centers, spas, and swimming pools. Select from a range of suites and room types to fit your needs and budget.

2. Bed and Breakfasts: Savor the charm and friendliness of lodging in a bed and breakfast, where you can look forward to individualized attention, quaint accommodations, and freshly prepared breakfasts. Explore quaint B&Bs housed in historic buildings, beachside cottages, and rural getaways to have a special and personalized hotel experience.

3. Vacation Rentals: Take advantage of the ease and flexibility that come with renting an apartment, condo, or vacation home in California. Look into the rental options offered by websites like Booking.com, Airbnb, and VRBO. You can select from a range of properties, including beachfront villas, lofts in the city, and cabins in the mountains.

4. Hostels and Low-Cost Accommodations: Stay in hostels and low-cost lodgings in California's major cities and backpacker hotspots to save money on travel and make new friends. Find reasonably priced private rooms, communal areas, and dorm-style lodging where you can make new friends and talk about your travels.

5. Camping and RV Parks: Camp in California's state parks, national parks, and wilderness areas to get a true sense of the outdoors and to fully immerse yourself in nature. Discover campgrounds and RV parks that provide a variety of facilities, including picnic areas, restrooms, showers, and RV hookups. You can also engage in outdoor activities like stargazing, hiking, and fishing at these locations.

6. Unusual and Unique lodging: Make your trip even more memorable by booking a stay in one of California's many unusual and unique lodging options, which range from treehouses and yurts to glamping tents and vintage Airstream trailers. Discover off-the-grid retreats, themed hotels, and eco-lodges that provide a unique lodging experience and help you make lifelong memories.

7. Tips for Booking and Reservations
Learn useful tips and strategies for making hotel reservations in California, such as how to look into options, compare costs and features, and read other travelers' reviews. When making reservations, take into account things like location, distance from attractions, cancellation policies, and exclusive deals. Also, make sure to book well in advance during holidays and popular travel periods.

Consider the variety of lodging choices that can be found all over California, as well as the chances they present for leisure, relaxation, and acclimatization to the local way of life.
When selecting lodging, take into account your preferences, financial situation, and preferred mode of transportation. During your California adventure, seize the chance to explore new and fascinating locations to call home.

Let this chapter's information and advice serve as a guide to help you choose the ideal lodging options for your needs and preferences as you set out on your journey through California. California provides an abundance of options to ensure your stay is truly unforgettable, regardless of your preferences for luxury and comfort, charm and hospitality, or adventure and exploration.

• Weather and Climate

To fully plan and enjoy your journey as you explore the vast and varied landscapes of California, it is imperative to understand the weather and climate patterns of the various regions. This chapter explores the various weather and climate features found in California, ranging from towering mountains and lush forests to coastal beaches and arid deserts.

1. Coastal Regions: Take in the cool summers, mild winters, and regular marine layer fog that characterize California's mild and temperate climate. Find out about the microclimates that exist along the coast, where temperatures can vary greatly from north to south and affect the weather in places like San Diego, Los Angeles, and San Francisco.

2. Desert Regions: Take a tour of California's interior desert regions, where daytime highs can reach triple figures and nighttime lows can be extremely low. Learn about the distinct ecosystems found in deserts like Death Valley, Joshua Tree, and the Mojave Desert. Be ready for intense heat and dry weather, particularly in the summer.

3. Mountainous Areas: Take a vacation to California's chilly and revitalizing mountainous areas, which are home to snow-capped peaks, alpine meadows, and pure lakes. Acquire knowledge about the various climate zones present in the Sierra Nevada, Cascade Range, and additional mountain ranges. Additionally, get ready for variable weather conditions, such as higher altitude thunderstorms and snowstorms.

4. Mediterranean Climate: Savor the warm, dry summers and mild, rainy winters that make California's wine country and Central Coast regions perfect for outdoor activities and grape growing. Discover vineyards, charming seaside towns, and picturesque scenery. Take part in outdoor pursuits like hiking, beachcombing, and wine tasting all year long.

5. Extreme Weather Events: Be ready for the possibility of experiencing extreme weather events in California, especially during the dry season and hot spells. These events include wildfires, droughts, floods, and heatwaves.
Make sure you are aware of emergency alerts, evacuation protocols, and weather forecasts. You should also take preventative measures to make sure you are safe and secure during bad weather.

6. Seasonal Variations: Plan your travels taking into account the weather and climate variations that occur throughout California throughout the wet season (winter and spring) and dry season (summer and fall). Take part in seasonal events and activities like harvest festivals in the fall, beach days in the summer, wildflower blooms in the spring, and skiing and snowboarding in the winter.

7. Advice and Tips for Packing and Preparation: Learn useful suggestions and advice for packing and getting ready depending on the weather and climate of your California destination. For outdoor activities, think about bringing layers, sunscreen, hats, sunglasses, and lots of water. You should also

be ready for unforeseen weather changes, particularly in mountainous and desert areas.

Consider California's varied weather and climate patterns and the chances they present for outdoor exploration, breathtaking scenery, and cultural immersion. When organizing your trip, take into account the climate and weather, and seize the opportunity to explore the wide range of ecosystems that combine to make California a genuinely exceptional travel destination.

Let this chapter's information and advice serve as your guide as you travel through California, helping you to navigate the state's varied weather and climate patterns. You can make sure that your trip to every part of California is safe, enjoyable, and unforgettable by being aware of the conditions ahead of time and being prepared for them.

• Health and Safety Tips

Prioritizing your health and safety as you set out on your journey through California's varied landscapes and energetic cities is crucial for an unforgettable and worry-free experience. This chapter contains vital information and advice to keep you prepared, safe, and healthy while you tour the Golden State.

1. Drink plenty of water. California's varied environment can cause dehydration, particularly in the summer or when engaging in physical activity. Drink lots of water throughout the day and carry a reusable water bottle, especially if you're biking, hiking, or spending time outside.

2. Guard Against Sun Exposure: Although California experiences plenty of sunshine all year long, prolonged sun exposure can cause long-term skin damage, heat exhaustion, and sunburn. To protect yourself from damaging UV rays, put on protective clothes, wide-brimmed hats, sunglasses, and sunscreen with a high SPF.

3. Engage in Safe Outdoor Activities: Always put safety first and abide by established rules and regulations when hiking, swimming, surfing, or participating in other outdoor activities. Keep to designated routes, swim in areas supervised by lifeguards, and be mindful of possible dangers like strong waves, rip currents, and coming into contact with wildlife.

4. Be Ready for Emergencies: Educate yourself on what to do in the event of an accident or medical emergency, including

how to get in touch with local authorities, hospitals, and emergency services. Always keep a first aid kit, emergency contact details, and any prescription drugs on you. Also, inform someone of your travel schedule and plans.

5. Drive Safely: Get acquainted with the rules of the road, traffic patterns, and driving customs in California before you rent a car or drive a car there. Observe speed limits and traffic signs, wear a seatbelt at all times, and steer clear of distracted driving to guarantee a safe and enjoyable drive.

6. Refrain from Risky Behaviors: California has a lot to offer in terms of nightlife and recreational activities, but it's crucial to abstain from risky behaviors like drug and alcohol abuse and binge drinking. While exploring new places, exercise caution and common sense and pay attention to your surroundings, personal property, and interactions with strangers.

7. Practice Good Hygiene: Especially in crowded or high-traffic areas, maintain good hygiene practices to prevent illness and minimize the spread of germs. When handwashing facilities are not available, use hand sanitizer, wash your hands often with soap and water, and refrain from touching your face with unclean hands.

8. Remain Knowledgeable and Adaptable: Remain up to date on any local laws or restrictions that might have an impact on your plans, as well as health and safety guidelines and travel advisories. Maintain contingency plans in case of unforeseen events and be nimble and adaptive to changes in conditions, weather, and circumstances.

Think about how important it is to put your health and safety first when traveling in California, as well as the comfort that comes from being well-informed and prepared.

Take into account the health and safety advice provided in this chapter as indispensable resources to guarantee a memorable, safe, and pleasurable trip across the Golden State.

Let this chapter's information and advice serve as your road map for traveling through California, helping you to stay safe, healthy, and ready for any adventures that may arise. You can fully immerse yourself in the beauty, culture, and experiences that California has to offer by putting your health and safety first, knowing that you're prepared to handle any situation that may arise.

• Useful Phrases and Language Tips

Learning some basic phrases and language tricks will help you make meaningful connections with locals and improve your travel experience as you immerse yourself in California's diverse communities and cultures. To facilitate your exploration of the Golden State and help you navigate conversations, interactions, and cultural nuances, we have included key phrases and language tips in this chapter.

1. Introductions and Greetings: Acquire familiar phrases like "hello," "good morning," "good afternoon," and "good evening," and practice utilizing them in various social settings. When you meet someone for the first time, remember to shake hands, look them in the eye, smile, and say something courteous like "nice to meet you" or "pleasure to make your acquaintance."

2. Basic Phrases for Common Situations: Learn some basic phrases for common situations, like placing an order for food and drink, asking for directions, and striking up a conversation with strangers. Learn how to say things like "pardon me," "please," "thank you," and "I'm sorry," as well as other standard expressions of appreciation and politeness.

3. Language Hints for Traveling: Review vocabulary that is pertinent to lodging, shopping, transportation, and sightseeing, and practice applying it in real-world situations.
Use translation apps or keep a pocket-sized phrasebook on hand to facilitate communication with locals, particularly in places where English may not be the primary language.

4. Cultural Sensitivity and Respect: When engaging with locals, respect their norms and customs and be aware of variations in language, demeanor, and manners. Steer clear of slang and colloquial language that might offend or be confusing to others, and modify your communication style to fit the formality and tone of the circumstance.

5. Embracing Multilingualism: Acknowledge the diversity and multiculturalism of California by learning the fundamentals of languages like Spanish, Mandarin, Cantonese, Tagalog, and Vietnamese that are widely spoken there.

Greet locals in their tongues and show interest in their history and culture to demonstrate your appreciation of cultural diversity.

6. Learning Opportunities: Make the most of chances to interact with locals and hone your language skills through immersive activities like language exchanges, cultural events, and neighborhood gatherings. When conversing with native speakers, don't be scared to make mistakes or ask for clarification; instead, view every exchange as a chance to sharpen your language skills.

7. Respectful Communication: When engaging with locals, engage in respectful communication and active listening. Additionally, demonstrate a sincere interest in learning about their perspectives, experiences, and tales. Speak inclusively, refrain from concluding stereotypes or preconceived ideas, and be open-minded to other people's perspectives and lifestyles.

While traveling in California, consider how important it is to learn some basic phrases and language tips to improve your ability to communicate and gain an understanding of local customs. Think of learning a language as a means of gaining access to richer experiences, stronger bonds, and a shared respect and admiration for the many communities and cultures that make up the Golden State.

Let the expressions and language advice in this chapter be your road map for successful communication and cultural immersion as you explore the diverse range of languages and cultures found in California. Embracing multilingualism and polite communication will help you build lasting relationships, promote intercultural understanding, and make treasured memories in the Golden State.

Chapter 4. Dining and Cuisine

- ## California's Culinary Landscape

Take a gourmet tour of California's varied culinary scene, where a fusion of flavors, ingredients, and cultures creates an experience that's unlike any other. This chapter explores the diverse range of cuisines, eating establishments, and culinary customs that characterize the thriving food culture of the Golden State.

Fusion of Cultures: Take in the culinary scene's variety as you discover how many cultures combine to produce inventive and one-of-a-kind meals in California.
Discover fusion foods, which combine traditional methods and ingredients with contemporary twists and international flavors. Examples of these are California cuisine, Asian fusion, and Cal-Mex.

2. Farm-to-Table Movement: Highlighting fresh, in-season vegetables and handcrafted goods, this movement highlights California's dedication to sustainability and locally produced resources. Learn about community-supported agriculture (CSA) initiatives, farmers' markets, and farm stands where you can enjoy the best of California's food and lend your support to regional farmers and producers.

3. Iconic Dishes and Regional Specialties: Savor regional specialties and iconic dishes that highlight the many flavors and culinary customs of California's various regions.

There's something to tempt every tastebud and sate every need, from clam chowder in San Francisco and fish tacos in Southern California to cioppino in Monterey and avocado toast in Los Angeles.

4. World-Class Dining Destinations: Throughout California's main towns and culinary hotspots, indulge in world-class dining experiences at acclaimed restaurants, Michelin-starred places, and celebrity chef-driven diners. Discover a variety of culinary specialties, cutting-edge tasting menus, and immersive dining experiences that push the envelope of culinary innovation and raise the bar for the art of dining.

5. Street Food and Food Trucks: Take advantage of California's thriving street food scene, where a wide variety of tasty and reasonably priced foods are available from food trucks, pop-up markets, and street sellers.
Savor the tastes of California while on the road by sampling gourmet tacos, artisanal burgers, ethnic specialties, and sweet delights from mobile vendors and culinary festivals.

6. Wine, Beer, and Spirits: Take a tour of California's vibrant wine, beer, and spirits industry, which includes artisanal distilleries, world-famous vineyards, and craft brewers.
Discover wine areas including Paso Robles, Napa Valley, and Sonoma County. Indulge in food pairings, excursions, and tastings that highlight the terroir and skill of California's concoctions.

7. Culinary Events and Festivals: Attend food and wine festivals, culinary contests, and gourmet events hosted all across the state of California to fully immerse oneself in the state's culinary culture. Join other food aficionados as you sample regional delicacies, get to know renowned chefs and wineries, and celebrate the diversity and richness of California's food and drink industry.

Consider the variety and depth of California's culinary scene, as well as the chances for exploration, learning, and sensory enjoyment it offers. Get ready to go on a gastronomic voyage that will excite your taste buds and leave you yearning for more. Think of the culinary experiences and customs covered in this chapter as a jumping-off point for your culinary excursions in the Golden State.

Allow the facts and observations in this chapter to take you on a delightfully fulfilling tour of the dynamic food culture of the Golden State as you relish the tastes and customs of California's culinary scene. A feast for the senses, California will leave you craving more, whether you're indulging in signature meals, finding hidden jewels, or venturing into uncharted gastronomic territory.

• Farm-to-Table Dining Experiences

Enjoy farm-to-table dining experiences that highlight the bounty of locally sourced foods, seasonal tastes, and artisanal workmanship to capture the spirit of California's culinary landscape. This chapter invites you to discover the lively culinary culture and varied agricultural landscapes of the Golden State, all while indulging in the freshness, quality, and sustainability of farm-to-table cuisine.

1. Embracing Sustainability: Get involved in the farm-to-table movement in California, where farmers and chefs work together to reduce food miles, support local agriculture, and promote environmentally friendly methods. This movement is based on a philosophy of sustainability and environmental stewardship. Discover the significance of biodiversity, seasonality, and regenerative agriculture in building a robust and sustainable food system that feeds people and the environment.

2. Making a Connection with Local Producers: Learn about the close relationships that exist between chefs and producers in your area. Chefs obtain ingredients directly from farmers, ranchers, and craftsmen to highlight the freshest and most delicious items available. These relationships are what makes dining at a farm-to-table experience unique.
Make meaningful connections with the people who cultivate and create your food by going to farmers' markets, meeting with growers, and taking tours of farm-to-table places. This will provide you insight into the origin and quality of the foods used in your meals.

3. Celebrating Seasonal Flavors: Savor the constantly evolving menu selections of farm-to-table establishments, which showcase the diversity and beauty of seasonal products picked at the height of their taste and freshness.
Savor the delight of dining through the changing cycles of nature, as menus change to reflect the abundance of California's agricultural calendar with a variety of fruits, vegetables, herbs, and meats.

4. Enhancing Culinary Craftsmanship: Recognize the talent and inventiveness of chefs who create culinary masterpieces that highlight the richness and nuance of California's customs and flavors using products that are produced locally. Taste the creativity and love that go into each meal as you experiment with new cooking methods, taste combinations, and presentation styles that bring out the best in farm-fresh products.

5. Fostering Community and Connection: As you get together around the table with loved ones and other food aficionados to share special meals and make enduring memories, take in the coziness and warmth of farm-to-table dining. Through shared experiences that feed body, mind, and spirit, support local businesses, encourage community resilience, and celebrate the interdependence of cuisine, culture, and location.

6. Organizing Your Farm-to-Table Experience: Look into local farm dinners, farm-to-table restaurants, and gourmet events. To guarantee a seat at the table, make reservations well in advance. To strengthen your ties to regional food systems and promote sustainable agriculture in your neighborhood, think about signing up for CSA programs, participating in farm-to-table dining clubs, or going on farm tours and seminars.

Consider the abundance and beauty of farm-to-table eating options in California, as well as the chances they present for social interaction, celebration, and gastronomic discovery. Think of eating at a farm-to-table restaurant as an adventure rather than a simple meal that allows you to experience the bounty and depth of California's agricultural history while fostering connections with the people, the land, and the stories that surround your food.

Allow the knowledge and ideas in this chapter to encourage you to embrace the principles of sustainability, seasonality, and community that characterize the farm-to-table movement while you enjoy the tastes and pleasures of farm-to-table dining in California. Farm-to-table eating delivers a taste of California's bountiful produce that is guaranteed to feed your body and spirit, whether you're dining at an upscale restaurant overlooking the fields, a crowded farmers' market, or your rustic farmhouse.

• Iconic Dishes and Must-Try Restaurants

Take a culinary journey across the varied culinary landscape of California, where mouthwatering cuisine and restaurants that are a must-try are waiting to tantalize your taste buds and stimulate your senses. We encourage you to discover the tastes, customs, and inventions that characterize the dynamic food culture of California in this chapter, ranging from ageless favorites to avant-garde culinary creations.

1. Savoring Culinary Heritage: Immerse yourself in the mouthwatering cuisine of California by savoring signature dishes that have come to define the state's culinary character. These iconic meals, which include the renowned In-N-Out Burger, the rich Cobb salad, the luscious California burrito, and the much-loved fish tacos, encapsulate the spirit of California's many culinary influences and regional flavors.

2. Must-Try Restaurants: Venture out on a gastronomic pilgrimage to some of California's most esteemed and well-known restaurants, where forward-thinking chefs push the frontiers of creativity and skill in the kitchen.
Find hidden treasures, celebrity chef-driven restaurants, and Michelin-starred establishments that highlight the finest of California's seasonal food, local ingredients, and international ideas for an extraordinary dining experience.

3. Coastal Cuisine Extravaganza: Savor the finest seafood, locally sourced products, and flavors inspired by the ocean as

you revel in the wealth of California's coastal cuisine, which defines the state's culinary environment.
Savor delectable seafood dishes such as buttery lobster rolls, creamy clam chowder, and beautiful crab cakes at seafood shacks, waterfront eateries, and seaside cafés along California's scenic coastline. Every mouthful is an ode to the sea.

4. Farm-to-Table Excellence: Visit eateries that promote sustainability, seasonality, and localization in their menus and sourcing methods to witness the farm-to-table movement in action.
Enjoy dining at farm-to-table restaurants that highlight the finest of California's agricultural wealth. Their menus are seasonal and contain products that are directly obtained from farmers, ranchers, and craftsmen in the area, guaranteeing a delightful and fresh dining experience.

5. Ethnic Enclaves & Global Flavors: Discover the thriving culinary neighborhoods and ethnic enclaves in California, where immigrant communities have authentically, passionately, and creatively brought their culinary traditions to life. Taste the tastes of the world colliding to create a gastronomic tapestry as varied as it is wonderful in areas like Little Tokyo, Chinatown, and Little Saigon. Suck into flavorful Thai noodles, aromatic Indian curries, and genuine Mexican tacos.

6. Street Food Sensations: Take in the diverse range of delectable dishes that California's street vendors, pop-up markets, and food trucks serve up, reflecting the state's innovative culinary scene and spirit of entrepreneurship.

You may try gourmet sliders, handmade tacos, fusion dumplings, and delectable desserts from mobile vendors and culinary mavericks at food truck festivals, night markets, and outdoor events by following your nose. This guarantees a fascinating and tasty street food experience.

7. Culinary Destinations & Epicurean Escapes: Arrange vacations with a culinary theme to some of California's best gastronomic hotspots, where you may indulge in gourmet experiences, farmsteads, and wineries to sate your palate and enhance your dining experiences. Take a gourmet road trip along the Central Coast, visit wine country in Napa Valley and Sonoma County, or indulge in farm-to-table feasts in the lush valleys of Northern California, where every bite and sip is a celebration of the state's culinary prowess and agricultural richness.

Think about how diverse and rich California's food scene is, and how much room there is for experimentation, exploration, and indulgence.

Take this chapter's list of must-try restaurants and famous foods as a guide for your culinary exploration of the Golden State, and get ready for a gourmet odyssey that will entice your taste buds, arouse your senses, and leave you craving more.

Let the knowledge and ideas in this chapter take you on a culinary voyage that honors the state's rich culinary heritage, unique flavors, and culinary inventiveness as you set out to discover California's signature dishes and must-try eateries. A feast for the senses and a voyage of culinary discovery that will delight even the most discriminating taste can be found in California's culinary scene, whether you're enjoying inventive fusion cuisine, traditional comfort food, or world-class gourmet experiences.

• Dietary Restrictions and Vegetarian/Vegan Options

Anyone may enjoy going on a gastronomic trip in California, even if they have dietary preferences or limits. This chapter looks at the variety of alternatives that cater to vegetarians, vegans, and those with dietary restrictions so that everyone may easily and happily enjoy the delights of the dynamic culinary scene in the Golden State.

1. Meeting Dietary Needs: California's restaurant industry is renowned for its flexibility and inclusivity, and a large number of establishments provide menu selections that may be customized to meet a wide range of dietary needs and preferences.
Without sacrificing taste or originality, customers may choose from a variety of foods that satisfy their particular dietary requirements, such as those that are low-carb, nut-free, and gluten-free.

2. Vegetarian and Vegan Delights: In California, where plant-based food is welcomed and cherished as a part of the state's culinary landscape, vegetarians and vegans are spoilt for choice. Discover eateries that provide creative vegetarian and vegan cuisine that appeals to both herbivores and omnivores. These restaurants include inventive recipes cooked with fresh, seasonal vegetables, plant-based proteins, and tastes inspired by across the world.

3. Farm-to-Table Emphasis: Due to their emphasis on using only fresh, locally sourced products and their flexible menu selections, farm-to-table restaurants are especially well-suited to satisfy dietary requirements and preferences. In addition to supporting local farmers and sustainable agriculture, diners can savor farm-fresh salads, vegetable-forward meals, and plant-based sweets that accentuate the natural tastes and textures of seasonal food.

4. Ethnic Cuisine Adaptations: With many traditional recipes being easily modified to suit certain dietary requirements, California's many ethnic cuisines also provide a plethora of alternatives for vegetarians, vegans, and people with dietary limitations. Discover ethnic neighborhoods and enclaves where you can eat vegan pho, gluten-free tacos, and other delicious, culturally inspired foods that respect the cooking customs of immigrant communities while satisfying modern dietary needs.

5. Conscious Dining Options: In response to diners' growing awareness of the effects of their food choices on their health, the environment, and animal welfare, Californian restaurants are expanding their menus to include more ethical and sustainable options.

Seek for eateries that give special attention to using organic, regionally grown food, endorse fair trade principles, and provide plant-based substitutes for animal products so that patrons may make decisions that are in line with their morals and principles.

6. Communicating Dietary Needs: Don't be afraid to let restaurant employees know about your dietary preferences and limits while you're eating out in California. They'll frequently be pleased to make special accommodations and provide tailored recommendations. To guarantee a secure and enjoyable eating experience, be proactive in inquiring about ingredients, cooking techniques, and any allergies. You should also not be embarrassed to speak up for your dietary requirements.

7. Community Support and Resources: Get involved in online forums and social media groups that discuss vegetarian, vegan, and allergy-friendly dining options in California. Members of these communities exchange advice, suggestions, and evaluations of eateries that may accommodate certain dietary requirements. Discover vegetarian, vegan, and allergy-friendly dining alternatives in California by exploring internet resources like restaurant directories, review websites and food blogs. These tools make it simpler than ever to locate delectable and accommodating meals wherever you go.

Consider how many vegetarian, vegan, and dietary-restricted alternatives there are in California's restaurant sector, as well as the welcoming attitude that characterizes the state's attitude toward eating out. Take this chapter's emphasis on vegetarian and vegan alternatives and dietary restrictions as a guide to help you navigate California's food scene with ease and enjoyment. Then, be ready to go on a culinary journey that honors taste, variety, and inventiveness for everyone.

Let the knowledge and perspectives in this chapter guide you as you explore California's food scene while keeping your dietary needs and tastes in mind, enabling you to make wise decisions and fully enjoy the flavors of the lively food culture of the Golden State. California provides a culinary experience that is as inclusive as it is wonderful, whether you're discovering diverse cuisines, creating your farm-to-table meal, or indulging in a plant-based feast.

Chapter 5. Nightlife and Entertainment

- ## Vibrant Nightlife Scenes in Major Cities

California comes alive at night, with big cities having thriving nightlife scenes to suit every kind of desire and taste. This chapter explores the vibrant energy, wide range of venues, and limitless entertainment possibilities that characterize major cities in California's after-dark scene.

1. Los Angeles: The Exotic Nightlife of the City of Angels: Explore the vibrant nightlife of Los Angeles, which offers a wide range of entertainment alternatives, including posh nightclubs, speakeasies, and live music venues, in addition to fashionable rooftop bars. PDiscover famous locations for nightlife, such as Hollywood Boulevard, Downtown LA, and the Sunset Strip, where you can mingle with celebrities, dance all night long to top DJs and see live acts by up-and-coming musicians in unique venues.

2. San Francisco: The Cultural and Culinary Center of the Bay Area: Discover the vibrant and varied after-dark scene in San Francisco, where a mingling pot of cultures, cuisines, and creative energy collides to create a unique nightlife. Explore stylish wine bars in SoMa, classic jazz clubs in North Beach, and fashionable cocktail bars in the Mission District. Here, you can enjoy artisanal wines, handmade cocktails, and small nibbles while taking in the lively vibe of the city.

3. San Diego: The Coastal Playground of Southern California Take in the laid-back atmosphere of San Diego's nightlife, which offers countless chances for celebration and leisure at waterfront clubs, beachside bars, and artisan breweries. Discover the exciting Gaslamp Quarter nightlife neighborhood, where hip clubs, rooftop lounges, and live music venues are housed in historic structures. The energetic atmosphere makes this area ideal for late-night exploration and bar hopping.

4. Sacramento: Hidden Treasures in the Capital City: Discover the hidden treasures of Sacramento's nightlife, which include live music, artisan drinks, and delectable food that come to life after dark in fashionable districts, historic sites, and local hangouts. Explore Midtown's unique bar scene, where you can enjoy craft beers in welcoming pubs, inventive cocktails in speakeasy-style clubs, and farm-to-fork dining at trendy eateries that highlight the best of Sacramento's culinary industry.

5. Oakland: The Cultural and Artistic Hub of the East Bay: Discover Oakland's exciting nightlife, which combines a robust music and arts scene, diverse neighborhoods, and cutting-edge food to create a lively and varied after-dark environment. Discover the city's warehouse district, where repurposed industrial buildings are the site of pop-up events, art galleries, and underground parties honoring Oakland's rich cultural variety and inventive spirit.

6. Santa Barbara: The Elegant Charm of This Coastal Retreat: Explore the sophisticated beauty of Santa Barbara's nightlife, which offers a taste of California's casual luxury and coastal elegance in wine-tasting rooms, premium lounges, and beachside pubs. Take a stroll down the busy promenade on State Street, where you can eat gourmet food, drink locally-produced wines, and see live music performances all against the backdrop of palm-lined walkways and expansive vistas of the ocean.

7. Planning Your Nightlife Adventure: Make a customized schedule that matches your interests and preferences by ahead of time studying well-liked venues, events, and areas in California's main cities. To experience the city's nighttime scene with local experts and other visitors, consider signing up for guided tours, pub crawls, or themed events. You'll learn about hidden treasures and insider recommendations along the way.

Consider the thrills, variety, and limitless opportunities of California's nightlife culture, as well as the remarkable experiences that lie ahead of you in the state's largest cities after dark. Take inspiration from the exciting nightlife scenes shown in this chapter for your nighttime explorations of California, and get ready to delve into an exciting and varied world of entertainment, culture, and excitement.

Let this chapter's knowledge and insights motivate you to explore California's bustling major city nightlife scenes, dance the night away, meet residents and other tourists, and make lifelong memories in the state's vibrant metropolitan centers.

California's nightlife offers an exciting and unique experience that will entice you to return, whether you're visiting underground art galleries, sipping drinks on a rooftop bar, or dancing to live music at a jazz club.

• Live Music Venues and Concert Halls

Experience the heart and spirit of the thriving Californian music industry at concert halls and live music venues that feature a wide range of performances, talents, and genres. We welcome you to explore the renowned stages, small-scale clubs, and landmark venues that make California a concertgoer's and music lover's paradise in this chapter.

1. Los Angeles: Epicenter of Musical Innovation: Immerse yourself in the vibrant music scene of Los Angeles, where storied venues and well-known sites have influenced the city's sound and culture for many years.
Discover iconic venues like the Greek Theatre and the Hollywood Bowl, where you can see concerts by well-known performers against the backdrop of the city's breathtaking cityscape and starry evenings.

2. San Francisco: Beatnik Soul of the Bay Area: Take in the unique music culture of San Francisco, where subterranean bars, small clubs, and historic theaters provide a stage for up-and-coming performers. Explore legendary locations such as The Fillmore, The Warfield, and The Great American

Music Hall, where you can get a personal look at the city's thriving counterculture and rich musical history.

3. San Diego: The Soundtrack of Southern California Discover the easygoing atmosphere of San Diego's music scene, where tiny bars, outdoor amphitheaters, and seaside venues offer the ideal backdrop for memorable events.
Get up-and-coming musicians at the Casbah, take in shows under the stars at the Humphreys Concerts by the Bay, or spend the evening dancing at the Belly Up Tavern, where each event is a celebration of music and community.

4. Sacramento: Capital City's Harmonic Haven: Explore the undiscovered treasures of Sacramento's music scene, where quaint cafes, old theaters, and neighborhood pubs provide small venues for acoustic gigs and live acts.
Discover places like Ace of Spades, Harlow's, and the Crest Theatre, where you can see touring performers, independent musicians, and local bands in a cozy, intimate setting that is characteristic of Sacramento.

5. Oakland: East Bay's Musical Mosaic: Explore Oakland's dynamic music scene, which features DIY spaces, underground theaters, and community-organized events that highlight the city's wide range of artistic expression and cultural influences. Discover the many sounds of Oakland at places like Yoshi's, The New Parish, and The Fox Theater, where you can groove to hip-hop, jazz, funk, and other genres in a lively and welcoming atmosphere.

6. Santa Barbara: Melody and Harmony of the Coast: Savor the seaside appeal of Santa Barbara's music scene, which has tiny clubs, outdoor amphitheaters, and historic theaters that present a variety of national and local artists against the stunning background of the ocean. Discover the allure of live music at locations like Velvet Jones, SOhO Restaurant & Music Club, and Santa Barbara Bowl, where you can take in the lively energy and carefree atmosphere of the city's music scene.

7. Planning Your Musical Adventure: Get tickets to your preferred shows and locations, as well as do some advance research on forthcoming concerts, plays, and events, to help you plan your musical adventure around California. Explore lesser-known venues, regional music festivals, and neighborhood cafés and pubs that provide live music every day of the week. Take advantage of the chance to find new music and performers in unusual places.

Consider the allure and diversity of California's concert halls and live music venues, as well as the part they play in forming the dynamic cultural landscape of the state. Take this chapter's list of legendary locations and small-venue clubs as a guide for your musical tour of California, and get ready to lose yourself in a world of song, harmony, and rhythm that is as enthralling as it is unforgettable.

Let the knowledge and perspectives in this chapter encourage you to explore California's live music venues and concert halls, seeking out new sounds, supporting regional musicians, and making lifelong experiences in the state's vibrant musical environment. California's live music culture offers an experience as diverse and dynamic as the state itself, whether you're rocking out to your favorite indie band, dancing to the beat of a drum circle, or swaying to the soulful notes of a jazz ensemble.

- ## Theatres, Comedy Clubs, and Performing Arts Centers

Enter the limelight and discover the allure of California's thriving performing arts industry at theaters, comedy clubs, and other venues that provide a wide range of artistic abilities, inventiveness, and amusement. We encourage you to discover the legendary locations, little theaters, and top-notch shows that make California a cultural hotspot for comedy and theater lovers alike in this chapter.

1. Theaters: Presenting Classic Dramas and Broadway HitsExplore the world of theater at the state's most recognizable locations, where Broadway blockbusters, vintage dramas, and cutting-edge shows come to life. Discover storied venues where you can see critically acclaimed shows, Tony Award–winning musicals, and avant-garde works by well-known directors and writers, such as the Pantages Theatre in Los Angeles, the Curran Theatre in San Francisco, and the Old Globe Theatre in San Diego.

2. Comedy Clubs: The Best Medicine Is Laughter Prepare to laugh out at the state's storied comedy clubs, where audiences

are treated to the wit, humor, and astute observational comedy of renowned comedians, up-and-coming performers, and improv troupes. Discover renowned comedy clubs where you can see stand-up acts, improv shows, and comedy showcases that guarantee nonstop laughter and enjoyment, such as The Comedy Store in Los Angeles, Cobb's Comedy Club in San Francisco, and The American Comedy Co. in San Diego.

3. Performing Arts Centers: Honoring Dance, Music, and Other Arts: Experience the world of performing arts at the top performing arts centers in California, where world-class artists, musicians, and dancers showcase their talents in breathtaking performances and cultural gatherings. Discover the wonders of symphony concerts, ballet performances, opera productions, and cultural celebrations that highlight the diversity and inventiveness of California's arts community at the Walt Disney Concert Hall in Los Angeles, the SFJAZZ Center in San Francisco, and the Spreckels Theatre in San Diego.

4. Small Theaters and Unusual Locations: Finding Undiscovered Treasures Discover California's big cities' dynamic and varied theater scenes, where small theaters, unusual settings, and experimental spaces provide one-of-a-kind, immersive theatrical experiences. Look for alternative theaters such as the Geffen Playhouse in Los Angeles, the La Jolla Playhouse in San Diego, and The Magic Theatre in San Francisco. These venues offer audiences cutting-edge performances, inventive new works, and shows that push the boundaries and excite them.

5. Arranging Your Cultural Tour: Arrange your tour of California's theaters, comedy clubs, and performing arts centers by booking tickets in advance for your preferred shows and locations and doing some advanced research on forthcoming productions, plays, and events.
Explore comedy shows, performing arts series, and themed theater festivals that provide selected programming and unique events all year long. Take advantage of this chance to fully immerse yourself in the depth and diversity of California's cultural environment.

Consider the diversity and vitality of California's comedy and theater scenes, as well as the ability of live performances to inspire, amuse, and unite audiences of all ages and backgrounds. Think of the historic sites and small theaters this chapter features as the starting point for your cultural exploration of California. Then, be ready to be enthralled by the enchantment, brilliance, and inventiveness that await you on the state's cultural stage.

Enjoy the knowledge and ideas in this chapter while you visit California's theaters, comedy clubs, and performing arts venues. It will encourage you to accept diversity, find new talents, and recognize the transformational power of live performance. California's cultural stage offers experiences that are both remarkable and enlightening, whether you're laughing at a stand-up comedy act, marveling at a ballet performance, or enjoying a Broadway musical.

• Rooftop Bars, Lounges, and Trendy Hangouts

At California's rooftop bars, lounges, and hip hangouts, you can take your nightlife experience to new heights. Stunning views, inventive cocktails, and a stylish atmosphere combine to create memories that will last a lifetime. We encourage you to explore the hippest rooftop locations and contemporary hangouts in this chapter, which provide a distinctive viewpoint on California's thriving nightlife.

1. Rooftop Bars: Enjoying a Drink and a View: Enjoy the ultimate rooftop experience at the best rooftop bars in California, where stunning views of the ocean, the city skyline, and the mountains make for the ideal setting for enjoying drinks and mingling with friends.
Discover popular rooftop hotspots where you can enjoy handmade drinks, delectable small plates, and expansive views of the surrounding area. Examples of these hotspots are Perch in Los Angeles, El Techo in San Francisco, and Altitude Sky Lounge in San Diego.

2. Chic Lounges: Mojitos and Discussion: Experience the chic and elegant atmosphere of California's fashionable lounges, where mood lighting, tailored playlists, and plush seating create the ideal setting for private conversations and elegant parties. Discover stylish lounges where you can enjoy fine wines, craft beers, and artisanal cocktails in a laid-back yet opulent setting that's ideal for capping off a night out or relaxing after a long day. Examples of these lounges are

Raised by Wolves in San Diego, The Bungalow in Santa Monica, and Bar Agricole in San Francisco.

3. Trendy Hangouts: Where Casual and Cool Collide: Accept the effortlessly cool ambiance of California's trendiest hangouts, which combine inventive food, fashionable décor, and a diverse range of patrons to create a lively and interesting setting. Discover stylish places where you can meet locals, try inventive cocktails, and take in the bustling, hip vibe of California's cities, such as Zeitgeist in San Francisco, Polite Provisions in San Diego, and The Standard in Los Angeles.

4. Sky-High Views and Sunset Soirées: Rooftop bars and lounges that provide prime views of the golden hour and glittering city lights are the perfect places to take in the allure of California's sky-high vistas and sunset soirées. When visiting locations like SkyBar in Los Angeles, The View Lounge in San Francisco, and The Nolen in San Diego, schedule your visit around sunset. These are great places to have cocktails, take pictures, and take in the splendor of the California sky as it changes from day to night.

5. Planning Your Elevated Experience: Make sure your visit to California's rooftop bars, lounges, and hip hangouts is easy and delightful by planning and studying dress rules, reservation procedures, and opening hours.

To avoid crowds and lengthy waits, think about going during the off-peak hours or on weekdays. Also, don't forget to check the weather forecast to make sure you'll have clear skies and the best views from the rooftops while you're there.

Consider the appeal and thrill of California's fashionable hangouts, lounges, and rooftop bars, as well as the distinct viewpoint they provide on the state's thriving nighttime scene. Take inspiration from the sleek bars and rooftop locations featured in this chapter to create your own elevated California experience, and be ready to be amazed by the breathtaking views, inventive drinks, and sophisticated atmosphere that you'll find wherever you look.

Let the knowledge and ideas in this chapter motivate you to enhance your nighttime experience and make treasured memories as you visit California's rooftop bars, lounges, and hip hangouts against the backdrop of the state's breathtaking skyline and expansive vistas. California's rooftop scene offers an experience that's as fashionable as it is spectacular, whether you're sipping drinks with friends, taking in sunset views with a special someone, or mixing with the smart crowd at a popular hangout.

• Cultural Festivals and Events

Visit California's cultural festivals and events to immerse yourself in a world of vivid colors, throbbing rhythms, and rich traditions as locals gather to celebrate their heritage, variety, and common humanity. We cordially encourage you to get fully immersed in the rainbow of customs, civilizations, and life experiences that make up California's vibrant cultural environment in this chapter.

1. Festivals Honoring Diversity: At festivals honoring diversity, which bring together music, dance, food, and art to highlight the state's unique legacy, one may immerse oneself in the rich tapestry of cultures that call California home. Discover occasions where you may fully immerse yourself in the sights, sounds, and flavors of cultures from around the globe, such as the San Diego Multicultural Festival, the Los Angeles Dia de los Muertos festivities, and the San Francisco Ethnic Dance Festival.

2. Music and Dance Festivals: Live performances, seminars, and interactive experiences provide an insight into the variety of musical traditions and dance forms that are prevalent throughout California. Let the beat move you. Discover events where you can dance the night away beneath the stars, discover up-and-coming talent, and groove to the rhythms of world-renowned musicians, such as Outside Lands in San Francisco, Coachella Valley Music and Arts Festival in Indio, and KAABOO in San Diego.

3. Food and Drink Festivals: Savor California's varied culinary heritage and farm-to-fork philosophy while indulging your senses at these festivals, which provide gourmet experiences, wine tastings, and culinary pleasures. Enjoy the abundance of California's agricultural bounty by sampling artisanal foods, sipping local wines, and discovering the state's tastes at events like the San Diego Bay Wine + Food Festival, the Eat Real Festival in Oakland, and the Gilroy Garlic Festival.

4. Art and Cultural Celebrations: Take part in events that highlight California's inventive artists, thriving arts sector, and cultural customs to fully immerse yourself in the state's creative spirit. Attend art exhibits, get to know local artists, and take part in interactive seminars and demonstrations at events like the Old Town Temecula Art & Street Painting Festival, the San Francisco International Film Festival, and the LA Art Show.

5. Community Festivals and Street Fairs: Take in the friendliness and warmth of Californian towns by attending street fairs and community festivals, which unite neighbors in honor of regional customs, heritage, and culture. Take part in the festivities at occasions such as the San Francisco Cherry Blossom Festival, the Pasadena Doo Dah Parade, and the La Jolla Festival of the Arts, where you can take in the festive and family-friendly ambiance while watching live performances, perusing handmade goods, and tasting delectable street cuisine.

6. Planning Your Cultural Adventure: Make a customized plan that matches your interests and preferences by ahead of time investigating forthcoming dates, places, and programming for your cultural adventure across California's festivals and events. To fully appreciate the richness of California's cultural scene, think about going to events in various parts of the state. Also, don't forget to check event websites and social media pages for updates, ticket information, and insider knowledge.

Consider the abundance and variety of California's cultural celebrations and festivals, as well as the feeling of camaraderie, kinship, and festivity they elicit in both locals and tourists. Prepare to be enthralled by the beauty, inventiveness, and passion of the Golden State's thriving cultural scene, and use the festivals and events included in this chapter as a guide for your cultural tour of the state.

Let the knowledge and ideas in this chapter motivate you to celebrate diversity, welcome new experiences, and establish deep relationships with communities around the state as you explore California's cultural festivals and events. California's cultural festivals offer an experience that's both enriching and unforgettable, whether you're trying different foods, dancing to the beat of a drum circle, or appreciating works of art.

Chapter 6. Top Attractions

• Disneyland Resort and Other Theme Parks

Experience the thrills, enchantment, and hilarity that await guests of all ages at Disneyland Resort and other theme parks around California. Set off on an incredible voyage into the realm of imagination and excitement. We cordially welcome you to explore the magic, wonder, and adventure that characterize the top theme parks in California in this chapter.

1. Disneyland Resort: The World's Happiest Place Visit Disneyland Resort to immerse yourself in a world of fun and imagination where legendary attractions, cherished characters, and enchanted encounters combine to create lifelong memories. Discover the magical areas of Disneyland Park, such as Fantasyland, Tomorrowland, and Adventureland. Here, beloved Disney tales come to life via exciting and immersive attractions like Space Mountain, Pirates of the Caribbean, and It's a Small World.

2. A Celebration of California Spirit at Disney California Adventure Park: Enter Disney California Adventure Park and lose yourself in its enchantment and wonder, where the state of California is brought to life through unique experiences, engrossing attractions, and rich narrative. Visit attractions like Guardians of the Galaxy – Mission: Breakout!, Cars Land, and Avengers Campus to take on exhilarating adventures and

meet your favorite big-screen characters as you journey through the worlds of Pixar, Marvel, and Star Wars.

3. Universal Studios Hollywood: Film Magic and Exhilarating Rides: Venture into the center of Hollywood at Universal Studios Hollywood, where thrilling rides, immersive experiences, and behind-the-scenes studio tours combine film magic with heart-pounding thrills. Experience the thrill of The Fast and the Furious – Supercharged, where you may lose yourself in the action and excitement of your favorite blockbuster movies, the fear of Jurassic Park – The Ride, and the Wizarding World of Harry Potter.

4. Knott's Berry Farm: Wild West Adventures and Family Fun Discover the allure and excitement of Knott's Berry Farm, where exhilarating rides, enjoyable family attractions, and engaging experiences provide fun for all members of the family. Discover the imaginative world of Camp Snoopy, brave the twists and turns of roller coasters like GhostRider and HangTime, and travel back in time to the Wild West at Ghost Town, where you can fully immerse yourself in the history and legacy of California's pioneer days.

5. Legoland California Resort: Building Memories Brick by Brick: At Legoland California Resort, themed parks, interactive activities, and vibrant LEGO® bricks bring creativity, adventure, and limitless possibilities to life. Let your imagination fly. Discover the rides and attractions at Legoland Park with a LEGO theme, play and splash about at Legoland Water Park, and go through an imaginative world at

SEA Creatures Aquarium to learn about interesting marine creatures and ecosystems up close.

6. Organizing Your Theme Park Adventure: Arrange your theme park experience in California by ahead of time investigating ticket choices, park hours, and special events. Then, make a customized plan that will make the most of your time and pleasure. To avoid the crowds and save costs, think about buying tickets online or from accredited merchants. Additionally, keep an eye out on park websites and social media pages for news, special offers, and insider information.

Consider the happiness, mirth, and memories that guests from all over the world make when they visit California's top theme parks—as well as the enchantment, wonder, and adventure they provide. To experience the excitement, thrills, and magic that await you at every turn, use the theme parks and attractions included in this chapter as a starting point for your unique journey in California.

Allow the knowledge and insights in this chapter to motivate you to go off on an amazing excursion into the world of excitement, creativity, and adventure as you visit Universal Studios Hollywood, Disneyland Resort, and other theme parks around California. Whether you're riding a roller coaster through the sky, seeing your favorite characters, or taking in breathtaking performances and activities, California's theme parks guarantee an experience that's both enchanting and remarkable.

• Golden Gate Bridge and San Francisco Landmarks

Discover the famous sites that characterize San Francisco's skyline, culture, and energy as you go into the city's center. We cordially invite you to discover the breathtaking splendor of the Golden Gate Bridge and other noteworthy sites that contribute to San Francisco's appeal as a tourist destination for people all over the world in this chapter.

1. Golden Gate Bridge: A marvel of engineering and a symbol of San Francisco Admire the magnificent Golden Gate Bridge, an engineering feat and a recognizable image of San Francisco that crosses the bay entry.
Discover the bridge's building and history. Known for its elegant Art Deco style and striking orange hue, the bridge was first inaugurated in 1937 and is now one of the most photographed and recognizable structures worldwide.

2. Alcatraz Island: The Historic Penitentiary and the Rock Visit "The Rock," Alcatraz Island, and take a tour of this historic prison that previously held some of the most infamous criminals in American history, such as Al Capone and "Machine Gun" Kelly.
Discover the rich history of the island as a military fortification, federal penitentiary, and Native American habitation site by going on a guided tour of the jail cells and visiting the prison yard.

3. Fisherman's Wharf: An iconic waterfront and gastronomic destination: Discover the lively waterfront neighborhood of

Fisherman's Wharf, which is home to seafood eateries, gift stores, and waterfront attractions, and take in its colorful vibrancy and historic beauty.
Take enjoy expansive views of the bay and Alcatraz Island from Aquatic Park Pier, peruse the stalls of Pier 39's well-known sea lions, and sample fresh seafood at outdoor crab vendors.

4. Union Square: A Shopping Mecca and Cultural Center: Union Square is a buzzing center of luxury shops, department stores, and art galleries. It is San Francisco's top shopping destination. Take in the sights at the neighboring theaters and music halls, shop till you drop at famous retailers like Macy's and Neiman Marcus, and take in works of public art like the Dewey Monument and Heart Sculpture.

5. Chinatown: A Dynamic Community and Cultural Hub Experience the sights, sounds, and smells of San Francisco's Chinatown, which is home to busy marketplaces, temples, and dim sum restaurants. It is the largest and oldest Chinatown in North America.
Explore traditional Chinese medicinal shops, meander through vibrant alleyways, and savor regional food at cafes to experience Chinese flavors without ever leaving the city.

6. The Painted Ladies: Victorian Architecture and Postcard Views Take in the sight of the recognizable Painted Ladies, a line of vibrant Victorian homes that border Alamo Square and symbolize San Francisco's architectural appeal.
Take a stroll around the park, and capture the beauty and history of one of San Francisco's most renowned sites in shots

with the lovely residences against the backdrop of the city skyline.

7. Planning Your San Francisco Adventure: Make a customized schedule that matches your interests and preferences by ahead of time investigating transit choices, attraction hours, and ticket pricing. To avoid waiting in line at famous sites and save money on entry costs, think about getting a city pass or attraction package. Additionally, keep an eye on local event calendars and weather predictions for updates and insider information.
Consider the awe, adventure, and feeling of discovery that San Francisco's famous sites arouse in tourists from all over the world, as well as its beauty, history, and diversity.
Awe-inspiring sights, culture, and vibes await you in the City by the Bay; use the monuments and attractions included in this chapter as a guide for your tour of the city.

Allow the knowledge and observations in this chapter to motivate you to go out on a voyage of exploration, adventure, and amazement as you visit the Golden Gate Bridge, Alcatraz Island, and other famous San Francisco monuments. San Francisco's monuments guarantee an experience that's as iconic as it is unforgettable, whether you're wandering through the bustling alleyways of Chinatown, discovering the ancient depths of Alcatraz, or taking in the expansive vistas from the bridge.

• Hollywood Walk of Fame and Studio Tours

Take a stroll down the recognizable Walk of Fame and take advantage of behind-the-scenes studio visits to get a look into the world of filmmaking magic and immerse yourself in the glitz, glamor, and history of Hollywood. We encourage you to tour Hollywood's star-studded pavements and travel behind the scenes to learn the secrets of Tinseltown's storied studios in this chapter.

1. The Hollywood Walk of Fame: A Place of Starshine Discover the charm of the Hollywood Walk of Fame, a renowned site that celebrates the accomplishments of the biggest names in entertainment with over 2,600 brass stars set into the pavement along Vine Street and Hollywood Boulevard. Enjoy a stroll along the Hollywood Walk of Fame and find the names of your favorite performers, singers, directors, and other icons of entertainment, honored with stars that honor their accomplishments in theater, music, cinema, and television.

2. Studio Tours: The Magic of Film Behind the Scenes: Experience the magic of filmmaking behind the scenes with studio tours that provide a unique look into the inner workings of Hollywood's storied soundstages, backlots, and studios. Explore renowned filming sites, historic sets, and interactive exhibits that bring the magic of the silver screen to life at Warner Bros. Studio, Universal Studios Hollywood, and Paramount Pictures. You can even take guided tours of these studios.

3. Hollywood History and Landmarks: Visit famous sites that encapsulate the glamour and essence of Hollywood to fully immerse yourself in the city's rich cultural legacy.
Visit iconic venues like the Dolby Theatre and the TCL Chinese Theatre, where red-carpet events, movie premieres, and the Academy Awards have created cinematic history. You can also visit museums that highlight the craft, technology, and appeal of filmmaking, like the Hollywood Museum and the Museum of Illusions.

4. Celebrity Homes & Sightseeing Tours: Take a guided tour of the homes, haunts, and neighborhoods of Hollywood's top stars to get a taste of the lifestyle of the stars. Take a trip around Hollywood Hills, get on a celebrity mansions tour, and take pictures of famous sites like the Hollywood Sign, the Griffith Observatory, and the Hollywood Bowl, where you can get sweeping views of the city and the famous Hollywood skyline.

5. Planning Your Hollywood trip: To guarantee your seat on popular tours and attractions, plan your Hollywood trip by doing prior research on tour alternatives, ticket costs, and availability. Make reservations as soon as possible.
A Walk of Fame trip followed by a studio visit or a sightseeing tour with stops at famous Hollywood locations are examples of mixing various experiences into one itinerary. Additionally, don't forget to check tour websites and reviews for insider advice and recommendations.

Think about the surprise, excitement, and discovery that tourists from all over the world experience when they visit Hollywood's Walk of Fame and studio tours, as well as the enchantment, history, and magic they provide.
Take this chapter's experiences and attractions as a guide for your own Hollywood vacation, and be ready to be enthralled with the glitz, glamor, and thrill of Hollywood.

Allow the knowledge and ideas in this chapter to captivate you as you stroll along the Hollywood Walk of Fame and take studio tours of storied Hollywood studios, encouraging you to discover the rich legacy, culture, and mystique of Tinseltown. Hollywood's attractions guarantee an experience that's as exhilarating as it is unforgettable, whether you're strolling past the stars on the Walk of Fame, seeing famous movie sets, or getting a peek at celebrity residences.

• Yosemite National Park and Natural Wonders

Take a voyage of amazement and fascination as you discover Yosemite National Park and the astounding natural beauties that have made it one of the most famous and cherished travel destinations worldwide. This chapter invites you to experience the majesty of the imposing granite cliffs, tumbling waterfalls, and unspoiled wilderness that epitomize Yosemite's unmatched magnificence.

1.Yosemite Valley: Magnificent Beauty at the Park's Center
Discover the breathtaking splendor of Yosemite Valley, the jewel in the crown of Yosemite National Park and the location of some of the park's most well-known features, such as Yosemite Falls, Half Dome, and El Capitan. Hike along picturesque routes that lead to breathtaking overlooks, marvel at the towering granite cliffs that rise hundreds of feet above the valley floor and enjoy the sights and sounds of lush meadows and gushing waterfalls that dot the landscape.

2. Glacier Point and Tunnel View: Stunning Panoramic Views
Glacier Point and Tunnel View, two well-known viewpoints that provide expansive views of the park's most well-known attractions and natural wonders, are great places to take in Yosemite's expansiveness.
From these amazing vantage points, capture images of Yosemite Falls, Half Dome, and the Merced River in all of their magnificence, and revel in the majesty and beauty of Yosemite's unique terrain.

3. Mariposa Grove: Forest's Towering Giants Admire the lofty behemoths of Mariposa Grove, which is home to some of the biggest and oldest sequoia trees on the planet, such as the well-known California Tunnel Tree and Grizzly Giant. Wander around the peaceful grove and be in awe of the sheer age and grandeur of these old trees. People come from all over the world to be in awe of these towering presences of breathtaking beauty.

4. Yosemite Waterfalls: A Stunning Display of Nature Be mesmerized by the awe-inspiring exhibition of nature's unadulterated strength and beauty as Yosemite's waterfalls plummet down granite cliffs. Take in the breathtaking sight and sound of North America's biggest waterfall, Yosemite Falls, and go to lesser-known falls, such as Bridalveil Fall and Vernal Fall, where you can get up close and personal with the enchantment of flowing water.

5. Outdoor Recreation and Adventure: Take part in a range of outdoor activities, including hiking, rock climbing, camping, and animal viewing, to fully experience Yosemite National Park's natural beauty and outdoor adventure.
Discover more than eight hundred miles of hiking paths that meander through unspoiled wilderness; ascend granite cliffs with top-notch rock climbing routes; and sleep beneath the stars at one of the park's campsites to take in Yosemite's allure after dark.

6. Arranging Your Yosemite Experience: Arrange your Yosemite experience by making reservations for camping,

reading up on park policies, and designing a customized schedule based on your tastes and interests. To avoid crowds and take advantage of the milder weather, think about going in the spring or fall. Also, don't forget to check the park's website and visitor center for information on road closures, weather warnings, and special events.

Think of the grandeur, splendor, and wonder of Yosemite National Park and its natural wonders, as well as the amazement, inspiration, and camaraderie they evoke in tourists from all over the world.

Take this chapter's experiences and recommended attractions as a guide for your own Yosemite journey, and be ready to be mesmerized by the majesty, splendor, and enchantment of one of nature's finest works of art.

Let the knowledge and perspectives in this chapter encourage you to go out on an inspiring adventure of wonder and amazement in the heart of California's wilderness as you visit Yosemite National Park and its natural treasures. Yosemite's natural treasures guarantee an experience that is as stunning as it is unforgettable, whether you're trekking through ancient woods, looking up at towering waterfalls, or soaking in panoramic panoramas.

- **Beaches, Coastal Drives, and Scenic Routes**

Explore California's charming beaches, coastal drives, and attractive roadways that wind down the Pacific Coast as you set off on a journey filled with sun, sand, and breathtaking views. Explore the richness and splendor of California's coastal terrain in this chapter, from pristine shorelines and jagged cliffs to well-known monuments and breathtaking views.

1. Beaches: tranquility, sun, and surf Visit one of the numerous immaculate beaches in California for the ultimate beach experience. The state's golden sands, crystal oceans, and moderate waves entice travelers to unwind, rest, and enjoy the sun.
Experience renowned beaches including Zuma Beach in Malibu, Santa Monica Beach, and Venice Beach, where you can sunbathe, swim, surf, and engage in a range of water sports and leisure activities against the backdrop of breathtaking coastal landscape.

2. Coastal Roads: Beautiful Scenery Along the Highway Pacific Coast Take a picturesque drive along the renowned Pacific Coast Highway, which runs from Southern California to the Oregon border and provides unrivaled views of the Pacific Ocean and the coastal scenery. The Pacific Coast Highway is one of the most famous and stunning coastal roads in the world. Travel along narrow roads that follow the coastline, taking in the quaint beach villages, untamed cliffs,

and breathtaking views that highlight the richness and beauty of California's coastal landscape.

3. Scenic Routes: Enchanting Sceneries and Undiscovered Treasures Explore hidden treasures and enthralling scenery along California's beautiful highways, which provide countless chances for discovery and adventure with their meandering roads, expansive vistas, and quaint coastal communities. Discover areas like the Mendocino Coast Scenic Byway, the Big Sur Coast Highway, and the Sonoma Coast State Park, where you can take in the awe-inspiring views of towering redwood trees, untamed beaches, and craggy sea cliffs.

4. Coastal Landmarks and Attractions: Explore famous landmarks and attractions that highlight the beauty and charm of the Pacific Coast, from historic lighthouses and charming piers to breathtaking vistas and natural marvels. See famous sites like the Golden Gate Bridge, the Santa Monica Pier, and Point Reyes National Seashore to take in the expansive vistas, leisurely walk along charming promenades, and learn about the rich cultural legacy and history of California's coastal cities.

5. Outdoor Activities and Coastal Adventures: Engage in a range of outdoor activities, such as hiking, bicycling, kayaking, and whale watching, to fully experience the natural beauty and coastal adventures of California's coastline. Take a whale-watching tour along the coast to see migrating gray whales, playful dolphins, and other marine life in their natural habitat. You can also explore coastal trails like the Monterey

Bay Coastal Recreation Trail, kayak through sea caves and kelp forests in the Channel Islands National Park, and more.

6. Planning Your Coastal Exploration: Make a customized schedule that combines beach time, picturesque drives, and outdoor activities by ahead of time investigating beach access, parking possibilities, and trail conditions.
To avoid crowds and enjoy a more tranquil and laid-back beach experience, think about going on weekdays or during off-peak seasons. Don't forget to bring sunscreen, drink, and snacks for your day of exploring.

Consider the freedom, adventure, and discovery that visitors from all over the world are inspired to experience by California's beaches, picturesque roads, and coastal drives.
Take this chapter's experiences and recommendations as a guide for your own California coastal adventure, and be ready to be mesmerized by the sun-drenched beaches, jagged cliffs, and expansive views that the Pacific Coast has to offer.

Allow the knowledge and observations in this chapter to motivate you to go off on a voyage of sun, waves, and breathtaking panoramas along the Pacific Coast as you discover California's beaches, coastal drives, and scenic roads. California's coastal splendor offers an experience that's as refreshing as it is unforgettable, whether you're exploring hidden jewels off the main route, relaxing on golden sands, or driving along meandering coastal roads.

Chapter 7. Day Trips and Excursions

- ## Wine Tasting in Napa Valley and Sonoma County

Take a trip into the heart of California's wine country to indulge your senses and excite your palette. There, you will see rolling vineyards, renowned wineries, and wines that have won awards. We extend an invitation to you in this chapter to enjoy the tastes, scents, and friendliness of Napa Valley and Sonoma County, two of the world's most famous wine regions.

1. Napa Valley: Wine Country Elegance Personified Discover the pinnacle of wine country sophistication in Napa Valley, a gorgeous area renowned for its breathtaking scenery, opulent resorts, and esteemed vineyards that provide some of the best wines on the planet. Explore renowned wineries such as Domaine Chandon, Beringer Vineyards, and Robert Mondavi Winery, where you can take a tour of the vineyards, taste a range of wines, and get education from skilled vintners and guides on the art and science of winemaking.

2. Sonoma County: A Tradition and Terroir Tapestry Discover the rich winemaking legacy and varied terroir of Sonoma County, a picturesque area renowned for its quaint villages, undulating hills, and well-regarded wineries that provide a more accessible and relaxed wine-tasting experience. See family-run wineries where you can wander through vineyards, have personal tastings, and take in expansive vistas of the

surrounding area, such as Benziger Family Winery, Jordan Vineyard & Winery, and Francis Ford Coppola Winery.

3. Wine Tasting Experiences: Savor a range of wine-tasting adventures in Napa Valley and Sonoma County, ranging from informative seminars and guided tastings to food and wine pairings and vineyard tours that provide a more profound comprehension and admiration of California's varied wine culture. Discover the distinctive flavors, scents, and qualities that set each wine area and winery apart as you taste a variety of varietals and wine styles, from well-known favorites like Zinfandel and Pinot Noir to less well-known jewels like Cabernet Sauvignon and Chardonnay.

4. Culinary Delights and Wine Pairings: Take advantage of the award-winning eateries, cafés, and gourmet markets in Napa Valley and Sonoma County to complement your wine-tasting experience. These establishments highlight the area's abundance of seasonal, fresh produce and farm-to-table philosophy.

At Michelin-starred restaurants like The French Laundry and SingleThread Farms, savor farm-fresh cuisine matched with regional wines; alternatively, choose a more relaxed dining experience at quaint bistros, wine bars, and roadside cafes that provide delectable fare and friendly service.

5. Wine Country Tours and Transportation: Take use of guided wine country tours and transportation services to explore Napa Valley and Sonoma County. These services provide easy

and quick ways to visit the area's vineyards, wineries, and picturesque sights.

To ensure a secure and enjoyable journey through wine country, select from a range of tour choices, such as private chauffeured tours, group wine-tasting tours, and self-guided wine-country excursions.

6. Organizing Your Wine Country Getaway: Arrange your wine country vacation by pre-searching wineries, tasting rooms, and tour companies. Then, make a customized schedule that fits your tastes, hobbies, and financial constraints. It is advisable to make reservations for lodging well in advance, particularly during busy times such as the autumn harvest. Additionally, stay informed about upcoming events, tastings, and promotions by visiting vineyard websites and social media accounts.

Think about how Napa Valley and Sonoma County's natural beauty, kind hospitality, and award-winning wines make wine lovers and tourists from all over the world feel happy, content, and pampered.

Raise a glass to the life-changing experiences and memories that lie ahead and use the wineries, tasting events, and gastronomic highlights in this chapter as a guide for your wine-tasting journey across California's wine region.

Let the knowledge and observations in this chapter encourage you to savor the natural beauty, warm hospitality, and top-notch wines that characterize California's wine region as you visit the wineries and vineyards of Napa Valley and Sonoma County. Napa Valley and Sonoma County provide wine-tasting experiences that are both wonderful and unforgettable, whether you're sipping Cabernet Sauvignon while taking in views of rolling vineyards or having a relaxed picnic with a glass of Chardonnay.

• Exploring the Coastal Towns of Monterey and Carmel

Explore the quaint villages of Monterey and Carmel-by-the-Sea, where historical sites, breathtaking scenery, and creative flair come together to create an amazing coastal experience, as you set off on a voyage of coastal enchantment. We cordially encourage you to explore the distinct allure, customs, and scenic splendor of these recognizable coastal communities in California in this chapter.

1. Monterey: Marine Wonders and Historic Wharves Discover the historical wharves and underwater marvels of Monterey, a charming seaside town rich in natural beauty and maritime heritage. Take a trip back in time.
Stroll down Cannery Row, which was formerly the center of the sardine-packing business and is now a lively waterfront area with shops, eateries, and attractions like the Monterey Bay Aquarium, where you can discover marine life from all over the world and marvel at the marvels of the sea.

2. Carmel-by-the-Sea: Artistic Charms and Charming Streets Take in the storybook village of Carmel-by-the-Sea's charming streets and artistic attractions. This town has long enthralled artists, authors, and visitors with its fairytale cottages, art galleries, and panoramic splendor. Take a stroll down Ocean Avenue, which is lined with galleries, stores, and cafés situated in quaint cottages and old buildings. You may

also discover secret gardens and courtyards that contribute to the enchanted appeal of the town.

3. Scenic Drives and Coastal Views: From towering cliffs and sandy beaches to expansive panoramas that reach as far as the eye can see, Monterey and Carmel's rocky coastline and natural beauty are shown through scenic drives and coastal views. Enjoy a leisurely drive along the gorgeous 17-mile Drive, which runs between Pacific Grove and Pebble Beach. The trip offers stunning views of the untamed coastline, well-known sites like the Lone Cypress, and renowned golf courses that hug the Pacific Ocean's coastlines.

4. Outdoor Adventures & Nature Excursions: Enjoy a range of outdoor activities, such as hiking, bicycling, kayaking, and animal viewing, to fully immerse yourself in the natural splendor of Monterey and Carmel.
Embark on whale-watching excursions from Monterey's historic Old Fisherman's Wharf, where you can observe migratory whales, playful dolphins, and other marine life in their natural habitat. You can also explore beautiful paths like the Monterey Bay Coastal Trail and kayak through picturesque waterways like Elkhorn Slough.

5. Culinary Delights & Coastal Cuisine: Savor the wealth of fresh, local products and creative cooking of the Monterey and Carmel regions in the area's well-known restaurants, cafés, and seafood markets. Dine al fresco on farm-to-table foods matched with regional wines from neighboring vineyards and wineries, or sample seafood specialties like

clam chowder, fish tacos, and grilled abalone at waterfront restaurants and beach cafés.

6.. Arranging Your Coastal Getaway: Arrange your coastal vacation to Monterey and Carmel by pre-planning your lodging, meals, and activities. Then, make a customized schedule that takes into account your tastes, hobbies, and financial constraints. To experience the true essence of Monterey and Carmel, book lodgings in charming bed & breakfasts, boutique hotels, or historic inns. Additionally, don't forget to keep an eye on the local event calendars and weather predictions for information on festivals, events, and outdoor activities.

Consider the awe, relaxation, and inspiration that visitors from all over the world derive from the charm, beauty, and coastal attractions of Monterey and Carmel-by-the-Sea. Prepare to be mesmerized by the charm, culture, and beauty that await you in these renowned California coastal towns as you use the activities and attractions included in this chapter as a guide for your coastal tour in Monterey and Carmel.
Let the knowledge and insights in this chapter encourage you to go off on a trip of charm, beauty, and coastal attraction along California's picturesque coastlines as you visit the coastal villages of Monterey and Carmel. Monterey and Carmel provide a wonderful coastal escape, whether you choose to stroll along ancient wharves, take in artistic attractions, or enjoy seafood delicacies while overlooking the ocean.

• Hiking in Joshua Tree National Park

Venture into the arid wilderness of Joshua Tree National Park and discover the untamed scenery, ancient Joshua trees, and craggy rock formations that await. This chapter extends an invitation to you to put on your hiking boots and experience the wonder, serenity, and beauty of one of the most distinctive and well-known national parks in the United States.

1. Overview of National Park Joshua Tree: Introduce yourself to Joshua Tree National Park at the outset of your trip. This vast desert region in Southern California covers an area of over 1,200 square miles and is home to a wide variety of flora, wildlife, and geological marvels. Discover the park's many habitats, which include the famed Joshua tree forests, rocky mountains, and high desert plains. You may also learn about the rich natural and cultural history that has sculpted this desert wilderness over millions of years.

2. Hiking Trails for All Ability Levels: In Joshua Tree National Park, there are a range of hiking trails to suit hikers' interests and ability levels, from leisurely nature walks and picturesque vistas to strenuous summit climbs and backcountry expeditions. Explore well-liked routes including Ryan Mountain, Barker Dam, and Hidden Valley, which provide breathtaking vistas, unusual rock formations, and chances to see animals like bighorn sheep, desert tortoises, and vibrant wildflowers.

3. Iconic Landmarks and Geological Wonders: Take in the breathtaking views of the geological wonders and iconic

landmarks that make up Joshua Tree National Park's terrain, such as the enormous rock formations, intricate valleys, and old Joshua trees that have withstood the test of time. See famous locations like Skull Rock, Arch Rock, and Keys View to take in the breathtaking sunsets, and stargaze beneath the desert sky, and take in expansive vistas of the San Andreas Fault and Coachella Valley.

4. Safety Advice and Preparation: To guarantee a risk-free and delightful hiking encounter in Joshua Tree National Park, adhere to safety advice and be ready for the hard and merciless desert terrain, particularly in the sweltering summer months. While hiking, remember to bring lots of water, sunscreen, protective gear, and food and drink to remain hydrated and fed. Always let someone know your hiking intentions and planned return time, and be mindful of the desert's fauna and perils, which include rattlesnakes, cactus spines, and extremely high temperatures.

5. Leave No Trace Principles: Adhere to the principles of Leave No Trace to lessen your influence on the delicate desert environment and protect Joshua Tree National Park's wildness and natural beauty for future generations. Remove any litter, stick to established pathways, and show respect for the local flora and fauna by keeping a safe distance and causing no needless disruption. For others to have the same sense of amazement and awe that you experienced, leave the landscape exactly as you found it.

6. Planning Your Hiking Experience: Make a customized schedule that takes into account your hobbies, degree of

fitness, and available time while planning your hiking experience in Joshua Tree National Park. You can do this by beforehand studying trail conditions, park policies, and weather forecasts.

To avoid harsh temperatures and enjoy more pleasant hiking conditions, think about going in the colder months of fall, winter, or spring. Also, don't forget to check the park's website and visitor center for updates on trail closures, ranger programs, and special events.

Consider the wonder, serenity, and beauty of hiking in Joshua Tree National Park, as well as the spirit of exploration, adventure, and closeness to nature that it fosters among hikers and outdoor lovers worldwide.

As you go on your hiking excursion in Joshua Tree National Park, use the routes, landmarks, and safety advice in this chapter as a guide. Get ready to be enthralled with the raw beauty and desert enchantment that this wonderland has to offer.

Let the knowledge and ideas in this chapter encourage you to start on an adventure, a voyage of discovery, and a journey of connection to nature in one of the most distinctive and famous national parks in America as you lace on your hiking boots and head out to explore Joshua Tree National Park. Joshua Tree offers a hiking experience that's as unforgettable as it is magnificent, whether you're hiking through secret valleys, scaling steep summits, or taking in the ancient Joshua trees.

• Visiting Historic Sites such as Alcatraz Island and Hearst Castle

Explore the famous historic landmarks of Hearst Castle and Alcatraz Island in California as you go on a voyage through time and history. We cordially welcome you to explore the intriguing histories, priceless architectural features, and rich cultural legacies of these iconic sites that have enthralled tourists for ages in this chapter.

1. Overview of Historic Sites: Get started on your journey by learning about California's historic sites, which bring the past to life with restored structures, antiques, and narratives that provide light on the area's long history and cultural development. PppDiscover the importance of historic preservation and the part it plays in remembering and paying tribute to the figures, occasions, and legacies that have influenced the history and identity of California.

2. Alcatraz Island: The Rock of Infamy: Learn the dark past of this rocky outcrop in San p Bay, which was home to some of the 0most infamous criminals in American history, such as Al Capone and "Machine Gun" Kelly, during its 34-year federal prison existence.
Take a guided tour of the prison to learn about p0ppthe everyday activities on the Rock, the daring escape attempts and inmate demonstrations that have become part of its reputation, as well as the cell blocks, exercise yards, and guard towers.

3. Hearst Castle: A Symbol of Extravagance Enter the lavish world of Hearst Castle, a stately home set atop San Simeon hills and constructed in the early 20th century as a display of wealth, art, and architecture by newspaper mogul William Randolph Hearst.

Admire the opulent interiors of the castle, which are furnished with exquisite artwork, antiques, and mementos from Hearst's enormous collection. You may also explore the expansive grounds, gardens, and pools, which are reminiscent of the majesty and beauty of European castles.

4. Architectural Wonders and Cultural Heritage: Take in the architectural wonders and cultural heritage of Hearst Castle and Alcatraz Island, which, with their unique designs, architecture, and narratives, highlight many facets of California's history and legacy.

Compare the intricate craftsmanship and many architectural styles of Hearst Castle's Mediterranean Revival architecture with the practical correctional system reflected in the architectural elements and construction methods of Alcatraz's prison structures.

5. Visitor Experience and Interpretation: Guided tours, video shows, and interpretive displays that offer background information, viewpoints, and insights into the history, significance, and legacy of Hearst Castle and Alcatraz Island may all help you get the most out of your visitation experience.

Interact with friendly park rangers, museum employees, and interpreters who provide educational programs, interactive experiences, and guided tours to help visitors of all ages fully appreciate the tales and personalities of Hearst Castle and Alcatraz.

6. Arranging Your Visit: Arrange your visit to Hearst Castle and Alcatraz Island by checking ticket availability, tour schedules, and transportation details ahead of time. Then, make a customized plan that enables you to fully enjoy and take in each location's distinctive features and services.
In addition to checking the websites and visitor information for changes in operating hours, accessibility, and COVID-19 safety procedures, you should think about making reservations and reserving tickets well in advance, particularly during busy seasons and holidays.
Consider the significance, history, and legacy of visiting historic locations such as Hearst Castle and Alcatraz Island, as well as the sense of inspiration, connection, and discovery they arouse in tourists from all over the world.
Take this chapter's featured tales, buildings, and visitor experiences as a guide for your investigation of California's rich cultural legacy, and get ready to go back in time to an intriguing, luxurious, and adventurous period.

Allow the knowledge and ideas in this chapter to encourage you to set out on a path of exploration, introspection, and gratitude for the narratives and legacies that have molded California's past and present as you visit the historic sites of Hearst Castle and Alcatraz Island. Explore the stunning ballrooms of Alcatraz and Hearst Castle, meander through jail cells, or take in expansive vistas of the California coast; all locations provide an amazing and instructive experience.

- ## Outdoor Adventures in Lake Tahoe and Mammoth Lakes

Take an exciting adventure into the unspoiled alpine scenery, glistening lakes, and countless recreational options that await you in the wilderness of Lake Tahoe and Mammoth Lakes. Explore the breathtaking scenery, thrilling experiences, and adventurous qualities that characterize these well-known locations in the Sierra Nevada mountains in this chapter.

1. Introduction to Outdoor Experiences: Get started on your journey with an introduction to outdoor experiences in Mammoth Lakes and Lake Tahoe, where there are countless opportunities for exploration, thrill-seeking, and heart-pounding excitement. Discover the wide range of outdoor activities these locations offer, from hiking and mountain biking to skiing and snowboarding, and how they cater to all interests and ability levels.

2. Lake Tahoe: The Sierra's Jewel Explore the stunning splendor of Lake Tahoe, a glittering gem tucked away in the Sierra Nevada mountains that is a nature lover's and outdoor enthusiast's dream come true. Enjoy a range of water sports and activities on the lake's immaculate coastlines and glistening waters, such as kayaking, paddleboarding, and sailing. Alternatively, unwind on sandy beaches and take in the breathtaking views of the azure skies and towering mountains.

3. The Alpine Playground at Mammoth Lakes Explore Mammoth Lakes, the alpine wonderland that is home to a quaint mountain town encircled by towering peaks, untamed wilderness, and top-notch outdoor activity options. Explore the extensive network of hiking and mountain bike paths that meander through verdant woods, rocky areas, and alpine meadows. Alternatively, take on backcountry skiing, rock climbing, and mountaineering expeditions in the neighboring mountains.

4. Winter Sports & Snow Adventures: Take advantage of the many snow activities available in Lake Tahoe and Mammoth Lakes, which appeal to outdoor lovers of all ages and skill levels as well as skiers and snowboarders.
Take to the slopes in well-known ski areas such as Squaw Valley, Heavenly, and Mammoth Mountain, where you can enjoy expansive views of the surrounding mountains and valleys, cut fresh powder, and land huge air in terrain parks.

5. Scenic Drives and Outdoor Exploration: Enjoy the breathtaking scenery and man-made marvels of Mammoth Lakes and Lake Tahoe by going on scenic drives and exploring the area's many ecosystems and landscapes.
Admire the expansive panoramas, towering peaks, and immaculate alpine lakes that dot the terrain as you go along beautiful byways like the June Lake Loop and the Lake Tahoe beautiful Drive.

6. Planning Your Outdoor Adventure: Make a customized schedule that takes into account your interests, preferences, and available time while organizing your outdoor adventure in

Mammoth Lakes and Lake Tahoe. Research trail conditions, weather predictions, and recreational options beforehand. It is advisable to make reservations for lodging well in advance, particularly in high-demand seasons like summer and winter. Additionally, don't forget to stay updated on festivals, events, and outdoor activities by consulting local event calendars and tourist information.

Think of the thrill, beauty, and excitement of outdoor experiences in Mammoth Lakes and Lake Tahoe, as well as the sense of freedom, enthusiasm, and connection to nature they provide to nature enthusiasts and tourists from all over the globe. Prepare to be astounded by the beauty, excitement, and wonder that await you in these well-known locations by using the events, locations, and experiences described in this chapter as a guide for your outdoor journey in the Sierra Nevada mountains.

Allow the knowledge and observations in this chapter to motivate you to set out on an adventure, voyage of investigation, and discovery in nature's playground as you experience the outdoor adventures of Mammoth Lakes and Lake Tahoe. Hiking to breathtaking views, skiing new snow, or canoeing through glistening lakes—Lake Tahoe and Mammoth Lakes provide an outdoor experience that's both thrilling and unforgettably memorable.

Chapter 8. Technology and Innovation

• Silicon Valley: Birthplace of Technological Innovation

Venture into the center of Silicon Valley, where the spirit of invention, business, and technological progress has molded the contemporary world. We urge you to investigate Silicon Valley's history, culture, and influence in this chapter, which serves as the hub of the worldwide tech sector.

1. Overview of Silicon Valley: To kick off your investigation, here is a brief overview of Silicon Valley, a Northern California region well-known for its concentration of startups, technological businesses, and venture capital firms that spur economic development and innovation. Discover how Silicon Valley got its start in the middle of the 20th century when semiconductor firms like Intel and Fairchild Semiconductor set the stage for the development of the contemporary technology sector.

2. Tech Titans: Innovation Icons: Explore the world of Silicon Valley's tech titans, which includes illustrious businesses like Facebook, Google, Apple, and Tesla that have transformed how we work, connect, and live.
Discover the inspiring tales of creative founders and businessmen like Steve Jobs, Bill Gates, and Mark Zuckerberg, who turned their concepts into multibillion-dollar companies and revolutionized the computer, software, and consumer electronics industries.

3. Startup Culture and Entrepreneurial Ecosystem: Learn about Silicon Valley's thriving startup culture and ecosystem, which attracts ambitious innovators and entrepreneurs looking to bring their ideas to life and create the next big thing. Find out about the networks and resources available to entrepreneurs and startups, such as venture capital companies, accelerators, and incubators, which offer money, advice, and mentoring to help businesses grow and flourish.

4. Innovation-Promoting Research and Development: Explore the realm of research and development in Silicon Valley, where leading academic institutions, research centers, and business labs work together to push technological limits and address some of the most important global issues. Discover the most recent developments in biotechnology, sustainable energy, artificial intelligence, and machine learning. These fields are fostering innovation and influencing a variety of sectors, from finance and entertainment to healthcare and transportation.

5. Work and Play: The Lifestyle of Silicon Valley Discover the distinct way of life in Silicon Valley, where work and play frequently coexist alongside a vibrant culture of creativity, innovation, and work-life harmony. Learn about the thriving eating and entertainment scene, outdoor leisure possibilities, and arts and cultural scene that make Silicon Valley a vibrant and appealing area to live, work, and play.

6. Silicon Valley's Future: Contemplate the region's future as well as the potential and difficulties that it may present. These

may include concerns about economic inequality, diversity and inclusion, and ethical dilemmas in technological development.
Think about how new technologies like virtual reality, AI, and driverless cars can affect society and how Silicon Valley can keep setting the standard for a better future for all people.
Consider Silicon Valley's significance, history, and culture as the cradle of technological innovation. Also consider the spirit of potential, ingenuity, and teamwork that characterizes this vibrant area.
View the tales, observations, and teachings presented in this chapter as a window into Silicon Valley and the individuals and concepts that will continue to influence technology and society in the years to come.

Let this chapter's knowledge and ideas encourage you to learn more about the world of technological innovation, entrepreneurship, and creativity that distinguishes Silicon Valley as you tour the area. Silicon Valley offers an experience that is as exciting as it is informative, whether you're touring famous sites like the Apple Campus or going to a startup pitch event in Palo Alto.

• Tech Tours and Visits to Major Tech Companies

Take a tech tour or visit one of the leading tech businesses in Silicon Valley to experience an interactive trip into the center of technological innovation. We cordially welcome you to explore the inner workings of the most significant tech startups and giants in the world in this chapter, where you will learn about their cultures, inventions, and effects on the world economy.

1. Overview of Tech Tours: Start your investigation with a summary of tech tours in Silicon Valley, which offer guests the exceptional chance to enter the offices of top tech firms and observe firsthand the state-of-the-art inventions and technologies that are reshaping the world. Find out why tech tours are so well-liked by travelers, professionals, and students who want to have a better grasp of the IT sector and its ecosystem, as well as chances for networking.

2. Iconic Tech businesses: Learn about the well-known tech businesses based in Silicon Valley, such as Apple, Google, Facebook, and Tesla, in addition to cutting-edge startups and research centers that are advancing technological innovation. Visit the campuses and offices of well-known IT businesses to see cutting-edge facilities, speak with staff members, and discover the background, goals, and plans of the organization.

3. Experiences from Behind the ScenesGet unique access to events and demos that take you behind the scenes of some of

the biggest tech businesses in Silicon Valley, showcasing their newest projects, products, and ideas.
Take part in interactive workshops, ask engineers and executives questions, and see firsthand how cutting-edge technologies like virtual reality, driverless cars, and artificial intelligence function.

4. Startup Incubators and Accelerators: Visit incubators, accelerators, and co-working spaces that assist and nurture entrepreneurs and early-stage firms to learn more about the thriving Silicon Valley startup ecosystem.
Meet the people driving innovation and entrepreneurship in a variety of industries, from biotech and renewable energy to software and hardware, and gain insight into the possibilities and problems that Silicon Valley businesses face.

5. Networking and Professional Development: Make the most of the chance to network and grow professionally by attending tech tours and big tech company visits. You'll meet thought leaders, industry experts, and like-minded people from all around the world.
Participate in industry conferences, meetings, and networking events organized by prominent technology firms, industry groups, and community organizations to broaden your professional network, enhance your knowledge, and gain new skills in the ever-changing and rapidly evolving field of technology.

6. Arranging Your Tech Tour: To guarantee a smooth and fulfilling trip, arrange your tech tour in Silicon Valley in

advance by looking into tour possibilities, making bookings, and planning visits to significant tech businesses.

When choosing tech tours and visits, take into account elements like tour length, group size, and particular interests or preferences. Don't forget to confirm tour availability, cancellation rules, and COVID-19 safety procedures before making a reservation.

Consider the thrill, creativity, and educational possibilities that come with going on tech tours and visiting well-known tech businesses in Silicon Valley. Also consider the sense of wonder, inventiveness, and possibility that these experiences generate in both tourists and business people. Think of the knowledge, contacts, and experiences you acquired on your tech tour as priceless resources for your career and personal development in the ever-changing fields of innovation and technology.

Allow the knowledge and perspectives in this chapter to encourage you to discover the hub of creativity and invention that characterizes this vibrant area as you set out on tech tours and visits to significant tech enterprises in Silicon Valley. Silicon Valley offers an experience that's as illuminating as it is thrilling, whether you're exploring the Googleplex, going to a startup pitch event, or networking with industry insiders.

• Virtual Reality Experiences and Tech Museums

Take a fascinating tour into the world of virtual reality and tech museums, where innovative displays and state-of-the-art technology come together to highlight innovation in the past, present, and future. We urge you to explore the wonder, excitement, and educational opportunities that virtual reality and tech museums have to offer in this chapter.

1. Introduction to Virtual Reality: To start your journey, start with an overview of virtual reality (VR), a game-changing technology that uses headgear and interactive devices to let users immerse themselves in simulated settings and experiences. Discover how virtual reality (VR) technology has developed throughout time, from its early tests in the 1960s to the latest developments in hardware, software, and content production that have made VR interesting and accessible to a wide range of users.

2. Virtual Reality Experiences: Immerse yourself in the realm of virtual reality experiences, where you may travel to far-off places, enjoy exhilarating adventures, and engage with digital creations in ways previously only imagined in science fiction. Learn how VR is being utilized in fields including healthcare, education, entertainment, and architecture to alter the way we work, play, and learn. Experience a range of VR experiences, from immersive gaming and entertainment to educational simulations and training programs.

3. Tech Museums: Conserving History, Culture, and Prospects: Discover tech museums that utilize interactive displays, relics, and multimedia presentations to preserve and highlight the history, invention, and influence of technology. Discover how computing, communications, and other technological advancements have evolved to shape the modern world by visiting world-famous museums like the Smithsonian National Museum of American History in Washington, D.C., the Museum of Science and Industry in Chicago, and the Computer History Museum in Silicon Valley.

4. Interactive Displays and Practical Instruction: Visit tech museums to interact with interactive displays and hands-on learning opportunities. There, guests may investigate ideas such as robots, AI, and renewable energy via interactive experiments, workshops, and demos. Take part in educational programs, special events, and guided tours to get a greater understanding of the science, engineering, and creativity that go into creating the technologies that impact society and our way of life.

5. Virtual Reality in Museums: Learn about the fascinating new ways that virtual reality (VR) technology is being utilized in museums to augment traditional exhibitions and bring science, history, and art to life. Discover virtual galleries, archeological sites, and historical sites through immersive virtual reality experiences that take you to far-off locations and eras, giving you unprecedented access to the past in terms of sight, sound, and interaction.

6. Planning Your Visit: Make a customized schedule that takes into account your interests, preferences, and available time when planning your visit to virtual reality experiences and tech museums. This includes researching locations, operating hours, and ticket choices in advance. When organizing your visit, take into account things like age limitations, accessibility, and COVID-19 safety procedures. Also, don't forget to check the websites of the museums and the visitor information for changes in programs, exhibitions, and special events

.

Consider the wonder, excitement, and educational opportunities that come with tech museums and virtual reality experiences. Also consider the sense of inspiration, appreciation, and discovery that these establishments foster in visitors of all ages. Think of the knowledge, encounters, and experiences you had during your tour as priceless tools for your professional and personal study and discovery of the ever-changing fields of innovation and technology.

Allow the knowledge and ideas in this chapter to motivate you to learn more about the exciting world of technology and innovation as you tour tech museums and immerse yourself in virtual reality experiences. Virtual reality and tech museums offer an experience that is both educational and amusing, whether you're delving into a virtual world, admiring historical relics, or interacting with interactive displays.

• Start-Up Culture and Entrepreneurial Spirit

Take a tour through the vibrant world of start-up culture and the entrepreneurial spirit, where audacious concepts, tenacity, and inventiveness come together to produce game-changing solutions and upend whole sectors. We encourage you to delve into the enthusiasm, ingenuity, and determination that characterize the startup ecosystem and feed the aspirations of would-be business owners throughout the globe in this chapter.

1. An Overview of Startup Culture Start your investigation with an overview of start-up culture, a lively and dynamic setting defined by invention, taking risks, and tireless pursuit of growth and innovation. Discover the history of start-up culture, which arose in the 20th century in reaction to the fast growth of technology and globalization. Since then, it has grown into an international phenomenon that cuts over national borders and professional sectors.

2. The Entrepreneurial Spirit: Immerse yourself in the spirit of entrepreneurship that propels start-up culture, where visionary, driven individuals seek to solve issues, upend markets, and provide value via novel enterprises and business models. Examine the attributes of prosperous entrepreneurs, such as flexibility, resilience, and the capacity to view setbacks as teaching opportunities. Discover how these traits influence the course of an entrepreneurial career and lead to long-term success.

3. Start-costs, U, and P Ecosystems and Hubs of Innovation: Discover global start-up ecosystems and innovation hotspots where entrepreneurs, financiers, and support agencies converge to promote innovation, teamwork, and expansion. Explore well-known hotspots for start-ups, such as Silicon Valley, New York City, and London, and discover developing ecosystems in cities such as Berlin, Tel Aviv, and Singapore, where resources, talent, and money are readily available to spur economic growth and entrepreneurial endeavors.

4. The Growth of Technology Startups: Explore the emergence of tech start-ups, which are now associated with innovation and disruption in a variety of sectors, including software, e-commerce, biotech, and fintech.
Discover the inspiring tales of well-known tech start-ups like Airbnb, Uber, and Spotify. These companies began as modest, ambitious endeavors with huge ideas and developed into massive international conglomerates that completely changed the way we travel, buy, and consume media.

5. Diversity and Inclusion: Examine how important it is in start-up cultures, where a range of viewpoints, experiences, and backgrounds foster innovation, creativity, and problem-solving. Discover the many programs and activities that attempt to foster diversity and inclusivity within the startup ecosystem. These include financing possibilities for underrepresented founders and entrepreneurs, networking events, and mentoring programs.

6. Navigating the Start-Up Process: Learn from seasoned business owners and industry professionals how to

successfully navigate the start-up process, from conception and validation to launch, growth, and scalability.
Examine the tools and networks of support that are accessible to prospective business owners, such as online forums, podcasts, and instructional materials that offer direction and motivation during the entrepreneurial process, as well as start-up accelerators, incubators, and co-working spaces.

Think about the transformational power of start-up culture and the entrepreneurial spirit, as well as the chances, challenges, and excitement they bring to individuals, communities, and society at large. Take inspiration and empowerment from the experiences, realizations, and teachings in this chapter for your entrepreneurial path, and never forget that everything is possible in the startup industry if you have passion, tenacity, and a willingness to take chances.

As you immerse yourself in the realm of start-up culture and entrepreneurial spirit, let the knowledge and perspectives in this chapter motivate you to bravely, imaginatively, and resolutely pursue your own goals. Start-up culture offers an exciting and demanding experience, whether you're starting a new business, joining a start-up team, or mentoring the next wave of business owners.

- ## Sustainable Technology Initiatives

Explore the world of sustainable technology projects, where environmental stewardship and creativity combine to produce answers for urgent global issues including pollution, resource depletion, and climate change. We cordially encourage you to investigate the state-of-the-art projects and technology propelling the shift toward a greener, more sustainable future in this chapter.

1. Overview of Sustainable Technology Start your research by learning about sustainable technology, a quickly developing sector that aims to satisfy the demands of both the present and the future while minimizing its negative effects on the environment.
Discover the fundamentals of sustainability, such as the triple bottom line of social justice, economic growth, and environmental preservation, and how these guide the creation and use of sustainable technology projects.

2. Renewable Energy Solutions: Explore the realm of renewable energy solutions, which utilize technologies like geothermal, hydroelectric, solar, and wind power to provide clean, renewable energy and lessen dependency on fossil fuels. Examine cutting-edge methods for producing renewable energy, such as improvements in the efficiency of solar panels, wind turbine design, and energy storage technologies, which enable us to harness the power of nature in ever more efficient and economical ways.

3. Energy Efficiency and Conservation: Examine how important it is to reduce waste and energy consumption in sustainable technology projects since they are key factors in promoting environmental sustainability and mitigating climate change. Discover how to save energy in homes, offices, and other settings. Examples of energy-saving technology and practices include LED lighting, smart thermostats, energy-efficient appliances, and architectural design techniques that maximize energy efficiency and reduce environmental effects.

4. Sustainable Transportation Solutions: Learn about environmentally friendly and more eco-friendly ways to travel while cutting down on the air pollution and greenhouse gas emissions that come with driving a traditional car. Examine developments in alternative fuels like hydrogen and biofuels, public transportation systems, and electric vehicles (EVs). You should also look into programs that support active transportation modes like cycling and walking, which enhance public health and air quality while lowering carbon emissions and traffic.

5. The Circular Economy and Waste Reduction: Examine the notion of the circular economy, which focuses on minimizing waste and pollution via creative design, manufacturing, and consumption methods, as well as extending the useful life of resources through sustainable extraction and regeneration. Find out about programs to cut down on waste and encourage composting, recycling, and upcycling of goods and materials. You may also learn about campaigns to do away with

single-use plastics and to support environmentally friendly packaging options that have a low impact on the environment.

6. Green Building and Sustainable Design: Examine methods for green building and sustainable design that put occupant health and well-being in the built environment, resource conservation, and energy efficiency first.
Find more about green building certifications such as LEED (Leadership in Energy and Environmental Design), passive design techniques, and sustainable building materials that guarantee ecologically responsible building design, construction, and operation.

Consider how innovative efforts in sustainable technology may solve urgent environmental issues and build a more just, resilient, and sustainable future for all. Think about the contributions that communities, governments, companies, and individuals can make to the advancement of sustainable technological solutions and the promotion of constructive change in the direction of a more sustainable and greener world.

Allow the knowledge and ideas in this chapter to motivate you to adopt a more sustainable lifestyle and to support programs that foster environmental stewardship and resilience as you investigate sustainable technology efforts. Sustainable technology provides a better future for future generations, whether you're using renewable energy at home, supporting environmentally friendly transportation alternatives, or encouraging green building practices in your neighborhood.

Chapter 9. Museums and Galleries

- ## Art Museums and Cultural Institutions

Explore the fascinating world of art museums and cultural institutions, where immersive experiences, educational activities, and intriguing exhibitions bring creative and historical masterpieces to life. Explore the rich tapestry of human expression and history conserved and on display in museums and other cultural institutions throughout the globe in this chapter.

1. Overview of Cultural Institutions and Art Museums: Start your investigation with an overview of art museums and cultural establishments, which protect humankind's cultural legacy and promote variety, artistic expression, and innovation. Discover how museums and other cultural institutions help to promote appreciation, understanding, and communication across cultures and generations by conserving, interpreting, and showcasing artworks, artifacts, and cultural practices to audiences of all ages and backgrounds.

2. Masterpieces of Art and Heritage: Explore the world of famous pieces of art and artifacts that have been conserved and are on display in museums and other cultural establishments all around the world. These items date from ancient civilizations to the present. Discover the histories, meanings, and methods behind these enduring examples of

artistic and technical skill by perusing collections of paintings, sculptures, ceramics, textiles, and other works from a variety of cultures, styles, and movements.

3. Immersive Exhibitions and Experiences: Investigate immersive exhibitions and experiences that blur the lines between the real and digital worlds, bringing art and culture to life in fresh and fascinating ways. Interactive installations, multimedia presentations, and virtual reality experiences are some of the ways that these experiences engage visitors.
Take part in activities such as workshops, guided tours, and hands-on exploration that promote creativity, experimentation, and deeper connections with artworks, objects, and cultural traditions.

4. Education and Outreach Programs: Through lectures, courses, symposiums, and cultural events, museums and other cultural institutions offer education and outreach programs that give chances for community participation, enrichment, and lifelong learning.
Find out about programs that support cultural literacy and arts education in libraries, community centers, and schools. You may also learn about outreach programs that target underrepresented and underprivileged populations and work to improve the inclusivity and accessibility of museums and other cultural institutions.

5.Examine the conservation and preservation initiatives implemented by museums and other cultural establishments to

ensure that artworks, artifacts, and cultural legacy are preserved for the benefit of future generations.
Discover the science behind conservation and the methods used to preserve valuable works of human ingenuity and legacy. These methods include cleaning, restoration, and preventative efforts to minimize damage caused by environmental elements, pests, and human activity.

6. Encourage Membership, Donations, Volunteerism, and Advocacy for Public Funding and Support as Means of Supporting Museums and Cultural Institutions in Their Mission to Preserve, Interpret, and Promote Art and Culture.Look for ways to get involved in the lively and diversified arts and culture ecosystem in your neighborhood and beyond by volunteering, attending events, and advocating for museums and other cultural organizations.

Consider the value and significance of art museums and other cultural institutions as stewards of human creativity and legacy, as well as the part they play in enhancing lives, promoting understanding, and creating connections between many generations and cultures. Take into consideration the anecdotes, encounters, and recollections presented in this chapter as evidence of the ability of art and culture to uplift, enlighten, and bring people from diverse backgrounds together, as well as the lasting legacy of museums and other cultural institutions as cornerstones of civilization and stewards of human creativity and legacy.

Allow the knowledge and ideas in this chapter to encourage you to embrace the transforming potential of art and culture in your own life and community while you visit art museums and other cultural establishments. A stimulating and illuminating encounter that highlights the richness and beauty of the human experience is what art museums and cultural institutions provide, whether you're admiring a work of art, going to an event, or participating in educational programming.

• Science Centers and Interactive Exhibits

Set off on an enthralling voyage through the realm of interactive exhibits and scientific centers, where curiosity meets adventure. This chapter offers you the chance to explore the fields of astronomy, biology, physics, and more as you solve cosmic riddles and interact with interactive displays that vividly and immersively bring science to life.

1.An Overview of Science Centers Start your journey by learning about science centers, vibrant establishments that use interactive displays, instructional activities, and demonstrations to stimulate curiosity, encourage discovery, and advance scientific literacy. Discover the history of scientific centers, which have grown to be well-liked hangouts for families, students, and science lovers of all ages. scientific centers first appeared in the middle of the 20th century in response to the rising interest in science and technology education.

2. Hands-On Exploration: Step into the realm of hands-on exploration, where guests are encouraged to interact, adjust, and try out displays that explain scientific concepts and phenomena in interesting and entertaining ways. Discover displays that allow visitors to construct contraptions, solve puzzles that test the intellect, and ignite their creativity as they investigate subjects like electricity and magnetism, motion and mechanics, light and sound, and the natural world.

3. Astronomy and Space Exploration: From the secrets of the universe to the most recent advancements in planetary science and astrophysics, take a trip to the stars with exhibits and demonstrations that delve into the wonders of astronomy and space exploration.
Experience immersive planetarium displays and virtual reality experiences as you visit the surface of Mars, pilot a spaceship across the solar system, and take in the sights and sounds of the cosmos through interactive exhibits.

4. Biology and Life Sciences: Discover the diversity of life on Earth with exhibitions delving into the intriguing fields of biology and life sciences, which include the intricacies of human anatomy, complex ecosystems, and tiny species. Through interactive displays that model biological processes, highlight biodiversity hotspots, and emphasize the interconnection of all living things in our world, visitors may learn about genetics, evolution, and ecology.

5. Physics and Engineering: Discover the fundamental ideas of physics and engineering via displays that cover everything from the forces that control motion and energy to the technology that has shaped our contemporary world. Uncover the mysteries of the cosmos with these exhibitions. Engage with displays that illustrate ideas like motion, gravity, and friction. You'll also be challenged to design and construct your inventions using robotics, engineering, and small machines, which will spark your imagination and problem-solving abilities.

6. Education and Outreach activities: Learn about the educational and outreach activities that science centers provide. Through school visits, summer camps, and community outreach projects, these programs give chances for lifelong learning, inquiry, and discovery.
Discover how to inspire the future generation of scientists, engineers, and innovators by learning about programs that support STEM (science, technology, engineering, and mathematics) education and career routes, especially among underrepresented and disadvantaged populations.

As centers of scientific inquiry and exploration, consider the wonder, excitement, and educational possibilities that come with science centers and interactive displays. You should also consider the transforming power these places have on people as individuals, families, and communities.
Take into consideration the tales, encounters, and recollections presented in this chapter as evidence of the ability of experiential education and curiosity-driven research to foster a lifetime love of learning, critical thinking, and scientific discovery.

Let the knowledge and ideas in this chapter encourage you to embrace the wonders of the cosmos and go out on your scientific research and discovery when you visit science centers and interactive displays. Science centers and interactive exhibits promise an enriching and enlightening experience that celebrates the beauty and complexity of the world around us, whether you're solving cosmic riddles, discovering the wonders of the natural world, or developing solutions to pressing problems.

- ## Historical Museums and Heritage Sites

Take a fascinating trip through historical museums and heritage sites, where tales of ancient civilizations, cultures, and historical events are conserved and exhibited for the benefit and instruction of guests. We cordially encourage you to dig into the pages of history in this chapter and examine the rich tapestry of human experience and legacy on display at museums and historic places throughout the globe.

1. Overview of Historical Museums and Historic Places: Start your journey by learning about historical museums and heritage sites, where objects, records, and monuments provide as windows into the past, shedding light on the victories, hardships, and accomplishments of bygone eras. Discover the significance of historical museums and heritage sites in maintaining, explaining, and showcasing history to a diverse range of audiences, promoting mutual respect, comprehension, and communication between many cultures and generations.

2. Artifacts and Artifact Collections: Explore the realm of artifacts and artifact collections, which offer insights into the material culture and everyday lives of ancient civilizations, cultures, and people as well as tangible linkages to the past.

Discover how historical artifacts—such as pottery, tools, weaponry, clothes, and artwork—are curated, maintained, and interpreted to convey the stories of the people and events that influenced history by visiting exhibits that include these items.

3. Archaeological Sites and Excavations: Travel to these locations to see the remains of historic towns, temples, and monuments that provide insight into the way of life and cultures of the past. Learn about the stratigraphy, mapping, and surveying procedures used in archaeological excavations, as well as how archaeologists unearth and interpret historical strata buried beneath the surface of the ground.

4. Interpretive programs and living history exhibits: With the use of immersive and engaging experiences, living history exhibits and interpretative programs transport visitors back in time by recreating historical locales, occasions, and ways of life. Engage with costumed interpreters who depict historical individuals and showcase traditional crafts, talents, and activities from many historical periods. Take part in reenactments, demonstrations, and workshops that bring history to life.

5. Heritage Conservation and Preservation: Examine initiatives for historical museums and heritage places that are meant to be preserved for future generations. Find out about programs to conserve historic structures, monuments, and sites, as well as endeavors to transcribe and digitize cultural heritage items to guarantee their continued existence and availability to scholars, instructors, and the general public.

6. Education and Outreach Programs: Through guided tours, lectures, seminars, and special events, historical museums and heritage sites offer education and outreach programs that give chances for lifelong learning, enrichment, and community participation.
Find out about programs that encourage civic involvement and historical knowledge, especially among youth, and that include a range of audiences in discussions regarding the value and applicability of history to modern society.

Consider the significance and influence of historical museums and heritage sites in serving as stewards of cultural legacy and memory, as well as the role they play in conserving, interpreting, and presenting the past to enlighten, inspire, and teach coming generations. Take into consideration the anecdotes, encounters, and recollections presented in this chapter as evidence of the history and heritage's continuing influence as sources of knowledge, inspiration, and identity in the modern world.

Allow this chapter's knowledge and insights to motivate you to go out on your own historical research and discovery adventure when you visit historical museums and cultural sites. Historical museums and heritage sites provide an instructive and fascinating experience that celebrates the depth and diversity of human history and legacy, whether you're gazing at ancient relics, visiting archeological ruins, or putting yourself in the shoes of historical individuals.

• Contemporary Art Galleries and Street Art Scenes

Take a colorful trip through the world of modern art galleries and street art scenes, where artistic expression has no boundaries and the streets serve as canvases for creation. This chapter offers you the chance to fully engage with the vibrant and always-changing world of modern art, from the regal corridors of galleries to the busy streets lined with vibrant murals and graffiti.

1. Overview of Modern and Contemporary Art: Start your investigation with an overview of contemporary art, a broad and eclectic field that captures the complexity of contemporary life and the range of viewpoints held by artists today. Discover the many trends, styles, and topics that have arisen in reaction to the social, cultural, and political currents of the times as well as the development of contemporary art from the middle of the 20th century to the present.

2. Contemporary Art Galleries: Explore the world of contemporary art galleries, where innovative works of both renowned and up-and-coming artists are recognized and shown in carefully planned events and exhibits.
Discover the newest trends and advancements in the contemporary art scene by attending artist lectures, curated exhibits, and studio visits. Browse galleries that specialize in contemporary painting, sculpture, photography, video, and multimedia installations.

3. Street Art Culture: Take in the colorful street art scene that is thriving in cities all around the world. Here, artists transform urban settings into outdoor galleries as a means of self-expression and provocative, unexpected public engagement. Learn about the origins and development of street art in graffiti and hip-hop culture, as well as how it came to be recognized and accepted by institutions and the general public.

4.The artistic expression and storytelling potential of commonplace walls and surfaces are transformed into lively canvases by the beauty and ingenuity of murals and public art projects that decorate city streets, alleyways, and public areas. See famous murals by regional and international artists that encapsulate the essence and vitality of the towns they live in as you stroll through areas and neighborhoods that are well-known for their street art activities.

5. Social and Political Commentary: Take part in street art as a means of social and political commentary, whereby artists utilize their creations to question established conventions, ignite discourse, and promote change on a variety of topics, from gentrification and urban development to social justice and environmental sustainability. Learn about the importance of street art in promoting awareness, developing empathy, and enabling communities to effect good change by visiting murals and street art initiatives that tackle current social and political topics.

6. Preservation and Documentation: Take into account the difficulties and possibilities of keeping street art preserved

and documented as a fleeting and transitory art form, as well as the initiatives taken by artists, activists, and cultural institutions to uphold and honor street art as an essential component of our cultural legacy. Discover projects that use photography, digital mapping, community-driven preservation efforts, and other methods to record and preserve street art. You may also discover how street art festivals and events help to promote communication and cooperation between artists and communities.

Consider the richness, diversity, and inventiveness of modern art galleries and street art movements, as well as how they enhance urban life, encourage innovation, and advance cross-cultural communication.

Take this chapter's tales, encounters, and recollections as a call to investigate and appreciate the diverse array of modern art in all of its manifestations, from the quiet galleries of museums to the busy streets of our cities.

Allow the knowledge and ideas in this chapter to encourage you to appreciate the originality, beauty, and diversity of modern art when you visit galleries and street art settings. Whether you're exploring a gallery, taking in a mural, or finding a hidden treasure of street art in your community, contemporary art promises to be a thought-provoking and stimulating experience that breaks down barriers and opens our eyes to new ways of looking at the world.

Specialized Museums: From Aviation to Maritime History

Take a fascinating tour around the world of specialty museums, where carefully chosen exhibitions, interactive displays, and immersive displays bring unique collections and particular histories to life. We cordially encourage you to explore the interesting domains of aviation history, maritime history, and beyond in this chapter, as you learn about the people, inventions, and artifacts that have influenced these specialized subjects.

1. Introduction to Specialized Museums: Start your investigation with an overview of specialized museums, which provide in-depth knowledge of the history, cultures, and inventions of their particular industries, subjects, or topics. Discover the variety of specialist museums, including science and technology, natural history, aviation and marine history, and more, as well as the distinctive experiences they provide for those looking to delve further into their hobbies and specific interests.

2. Aviation Museums: Explore the realm of aviation museums, where the history of flight is brought to life via interactive displays, historic relics, and exhibitions including vintage aircraft that honor the accomplishments, inventions, and pioneers of aviation leaders in the field. Learn about the development of aviation technology, from the Wright brothers' maiden flight to the most recent developments in aerospace engineering and design, as you explore collections of aircraft

ranging from early biplanes and World War II fighters to contemporary jets and spaceships.

3. Maritime History Museums: Take a trip through these museums, where displays tracing the discovery, commerce, and navigation of the world's oceans and rivers bring to life the rich heritage of nautical cultures and traditions.
Discover the technology, navigational aids, and marine practices that have influenced human history and culture. You may also learn about the stories of fabled ships, illusive journeys, and maritime tragedies via the exploration of artifacts, models, and nautical artifacts.

4. Science and Technology Museums: Discover the wonders of human creativity and inventiveness at science and technology museums. From the most recent developments in robots, artificial intelligence, and space exploration to the most ground-breaking discoveries in physics, chemistry, and biology.
Take part in interactive displays and practical exercises that illustrate scientific concepts and phenomena. Discover the achievements of scientists, engineers, and innovators that have revolutionized our comprehension of the natural world and pushed the frontiers of human knowledge.

5. Natural History Museums: Explore the beginnings and development of life on Earth, from the emergence of prehistoric organisms to the birth of contemporary people, and the richness of ecosystems worldwide by taking a trip back in time with natural history museums.

Discover the processes of evolution, adaptation, and extinction that have formed the diversity of life on our planet over millions of years by coming into contact with fossils, skeletons, and specimens of extinct and endangered species.

6. Specialized Collections and Exhibitions: From medical museums and sports halls of fame to automotive museums and railroad heritage centers, discover specialized collections and exhibits that delve into niche subjects and themes. Cultural institutions that honor the histories and customs of particular communities and ethnic groups are also included. Discover the many tales, inventions, and relics on display at these niche museums, as well as the important role they serve in conserving, interpreting, and sharing with people of all ages and backgrounds the rich tapestry of human experience and legacy.

Consider the range and richness of specialist museums, as well as the distinctive experiences they provide for those looking to delve deeply into particular hobbies and passions.
Take this chapter's tales, encounters, and recollections as a call to action to go out on a personal quest of inquiry into the intriguing fields of aviation, maritime history, science and technology, natural history, and beyond.

Let the knowledge and insights in this chapter encourage you to learn more about the histories, cultures, and inventions that have created our world, and continue to arouse wonder, curiosity, and inventiveness when you visit specialist museums. A fascinating and educational experience that highlights the richness and complexity of human effort and creativity can be had at specialty museums, whether you're marveling at antique airplanes, diving into the ocean, or deciphering the secrets of space.

Chapter 10. Beyond the Guidebook: Insider Tips and Recommendations

- ## Hidden Gems and Off-the-Beaten-Path Discoveries

Set off on an exploration voyage as we explore the realm of undiscovered treasures and off-the-beaten-path finds, where excitement lurks around every corner and chance meetings are just waiting to happen. We encourage you to explore this chapter's hidden gems that are not commonly seen by tourists and to veer off the well-traveled tourist route.

1. An Overview of Secret Treasures: Start your journey by learning about hidden jewels, those undiscovered areas, and hidden riches that lie for the inquisitive tourist prepared to venture beyond the well-known tourist destinations.
Discover the appeal of hidden jewels, which can range from quiet oases and remote natural beauties to oddball landmarks, abandoned ruins, and undiscovered cultural treasures that provide a window into a place's true essence.

2. Seclusion Natural marvels: Get away from the throng and find seclusion natural marvels that provide a tranquil haven from the bustle of well-known tourist destinations. Discover undiscovered beaches, immaculate waterfalls, peaceful hiking paths, and secret caverns nestled in far-off regions of the globe. Indulge in the peace and beauty of unspoiled environments.

3. Adorable Villages and Towns: Venture off the beaten track and discover adorable villages and towns that provide insight into the enduring routines of the local way of life.
Explore ancient squares, cobblestone streets, and secret passageways where you may enjoy the small-town charms of colorful homes, quaint cafes, and artisan stores.

4. Unusual Landmarks and Interests: Discover unusual locations and oddball treasures that elevate your travel experiences and challenge expectations. Look for obscure sculptures, strange museums, side-of-the-road sights, and odd architectural marvels that arouse interest and amaze with their distinctive appeal.

5. neglected Ruins & Historical monuments: Travel back in time to discover historical monuments and neglected ruins that provide a window into the past and tales of long-gone civilizations. Explore overgrown trails, dilapidated castles, and deserted ghost towns to learn about the mysteries and secrets of the past that have been buried beneath years and layers of time.

6. Local beauties and Insider advice: Ask locals and other tourists who have visited the area in-depth about its hidden beauties for insider information on local gems and insider advice. Explore residents' recommended lesser-known sights, undiscovered eateries, and secret overlooks. Indulge in the genuine tastes and sensations that make a place genuinely unique.
Think back to the excitement of exploration and the awe that results from finding undiscovered treasures and discoveries

that aren't normally made. Think of the tales, encounters, and recollections presented in this chapter as a call to embrace the spirit of adventure and see the world with curiosity and an open mind.

Let the knowledge and ideas in this chapter motivate you to seek out new experiences and make lifelong memories when you stray off the beaten road and discover hidden treasures. Traveling to remote natural beauties, discovering unusual sites, or wandering through quaint villages—discovering hidden jewels ensures an unforgettable experience of wonder and exploration.

• Local Insights and Recommendations from Experts

Set off on a voyage of exploration as we explore the realm of expert suggestions and local insights, where insider information and firsthand experiences pave the way to genuine travel experiences. We welcome you to use the knowledge of seasoned travelers, cultural specialists, and local experts in this chapter as they share their insider tips, tricks, and must-see locations.

1. Introduction to Local Insights: Start your journey with an introduction to local insights, those priceless pearls of knowledge, and insider advice that provide a more profound comprehension of a location's history, culture, and undiscovered gems.
Discover the value of interacting with people, looking for genuine experiences off the beaten path, and the assistance of local experts in enhancing your travel experiences via their advice and knowledge.

2. Meet the Experts: Become acquainted with the professionals who will lead you on your adventure. They range from seasoned tourists and travel bloggers to passionate local guides, historians, and cultural ambassadors.
Learn about the events and tales that have influenced their viewpoints and thoughts, as well as the advice and suggestions they have to give for optimizing your trips.

3. Insider Advice for Genuine Experiences: Learn about insider advice for genuine experiences that engulf you in the local customs, culture, and way of life of a place, revealing its essence. Examine suggestions for off-the-beaten-path sights, undiscovered treasures, and cultural encounters that provide a closer bond with the locals and the areas you visit.

4. Culinary pleasures and Local food: Treat your palate to expert suggestions for regional food and culinary pleasures that encapsulate a place's gastronomic traditions and culinary legacy. Explore residents' favorite secret restaurants, food carts, and traditional markets. Savor the flavors of local specialties, home-style meals, and handcrafted treats that capture the distinct personality and flavors of a place.

5. Cultural Immersion and Meaningful Experiences: Connect with local communities and customs by connecting via real interactions and meaningful experiences that let you fully immerse yourself in a destination's cultural fabric. Take part in rituals, workshops, and cultural festivals. You may also interact with local singers, storytellers, and artists who can provide you with insights into the rich tapestry of their culture.

6. Sustainable Travel and Responsible Tourism: Adopt the tenets of sustainable travel and responsible tourism, and make use of professional advice to reduce your environmental footprint and boost regional economies and communities. Find out about volunteer opportunities, eco-friendly lodging options, and community-based tourism programs that let you

contribute back to the areas you visit and leave a good legacy for future generations.

Consider how valuable professional advice and local insights may be in improving your travel experiences and helping you forge lasting relationships with the locations you visit. Take this chapter's tales, insights, and suggestions as a roadmap for discovering the real deal when it comes to traveling and experiencing the diverse customs, food, and culture of the places you visit.

Let the knowledge and insights in this chapter encourage you to seek out genuine experiences and make lifelong memories that will enhance your journey and increase your appreciation for the world's diverse cultures and destinations as you set out on your travel adventures armed with local insights and expert recommendations.

- ## Sustainable Travel Practices and Responsible Tourism

As we explore the realm of sustainable travel practices and responsible tourism, set out on a path towards mindful discovery and eco-conscious vacations. We encourage you to travel with the values of sustainability, respect, and stewardship in this chapter to make sure that your trip has a beneficial effect on the environment and the communities you visit.

1. Overview of Eco-Friendly Travel: Start your adventure by learning about sustainable travel, which is a way of thinking and doing exploration that emphasizes social responsibility, environmental preservation, and cultural preservation. Discover the role that responsible tourism plays in encouraging ethical and sustainable travel experiences, as well as the significance of sustainable travel practices in reducing the negative effects of tourism, such as carbon emissions, habitat damage, and cultural exploitation.

2. Principles of Sustainable Travel: Learn about the principles of sustainable travel, which include preserving natural and cultural heritage, limiting your environmental impact, honoring local customs and cultures, and boosting the local economy. While traveling, get useful advice and pointers for cutting waste, conserving energy and water, lowering your carbon footprint, and assisting sustainable enterprises and projects.

3. Greenly Friendly Lodgings: Select eco-friendly lodgings that have an emphasis on environmental preservation and sustainability, such as eco-lodges, boutique hotels, sustainable resorts, and community-based homestays. Find out about green certifications and environmentally friendly policies implemented by lodging establishments, including water and energy saving, waste minimization, energy-efficient construction, and support for regional conservation initiatives and community development initiatives.

4. Responsible Wildlife Tourism: Take part in activities related to responsible wildlife tourism, with an emphasis on protecting and preserving species and their natural environments. Discover how to have ethical wildlife interactions by seeing animals in their natural environments, contributing to conservation efforts, and staying away from practices that hurt or exploit wildlife, such as taking pictures with animals and visiting confined animal attractions.

5. Cultural Respect and Community Engagement: Honor local customs, values, and ways of life by showing respect and interacting with them. Engage in cultural activities that foster mutual understanding and cross-cultural interchange, such as going to local markets, supporting artisanal goods and customs, and attending festivals.

6. Leave-No-Trace Travel: Follow the guidelines in Leave-No-Trace to reduce your influence on the natural and cultural ecosystems, leaving them in their original state for the enjoyment of future generations.

Find more about Leave-No-Trace guidelines, which include clearing away your trash, sticking to authorized routes, being mindful of wildlife and their natural environments, and avoiding disturbing cultural items.

Contemplate the significance of eco-friendly travel strategies and conscientious tourism in conserving the Earth's ecological and cultural legacy while fostering favorable social and financial consequences for indigenous populations. To help you make wise and moral travel decisions that protect the environment and enhance your travel experiences, take into consideration the values and strategies discussed in this chapter. With a dedication to sustainability and responsible tourism, when you set out on your travels, let this chapter's ideas and recommendations lead you to worthwhile and fulfilling experiences that will benefit present and future generations.

- **Community Engagement and Volunteer Opportunities**

Join us as we explore the world of volunteer opportunities and community involvement, where visitors can interact with locals, give back, and truly affect the areas they visit. It's a trip full of purpose and effect. This chapter invites you to explore the transformational potential of volunteerism and the power of community participation while you travel the world.

1.Overview of Community Engagement: Get started on your trip with an overview of community engagement, a travel concept that places an emphasis on deep connections with local communities and aims to promote good social change. Discover the value of community involvement in fostering intercultural understanding, bridging the gap between visitors and residents, and establishing enduring bonds that cut across boundaries.

2. Kinds of Opportunities for Volunteering: Discover the wide range of volunteer options that are accessible to tourists, including initiatives for community development, education, healthcare, and protection of animals and the environment. Find volunteer opportunities that fit with your beliefs and passions by researching programs that accommodate a variety of interests, abilities, and time commitments.

3. Benefits of Volunteering: Learn about the advantages of volunteering for individuals as well as the communities they support. These advantages range from sustainable

development and community empowerment to personal development and cultural immersion.
Discover the transforming potential of volunteering in promoting empathy, compassion, and global citizenship, as well as the positive effects of volunteer programs on local economies, healthcare, education, and environmental protection.

4. Locating Volunteer activities: Whether through charitable organizations, volunteer placement agencies, or grassroots campaigns, learn how to locate volunteer activities that meet your interests, abilities, and availability.
Learn how to evaluate and choose responsible and ethical volunteer activities by exploring internet platforms and tools that link volunteers with organizations and projects worldwide.

5. Connecting with Local Communities: As you establish connections based on respect, trust, and understanding with local communities, you will learn the art of community participation and cultural exchange. Discover the advantages of listening, learning, and working with local partners to co-create solutions that address community needs and goals. You will also learn about the significance of cultural awareness and humility while interacting with communities.

6. Creating a Lasting influence: Examine methods for using volunteers to create a lasting influence, such as empowering local leaders, fostering sustainable practices, and advancing social justice. After your volunteer placement is over, think back on the things you've learned and the experiences you've

shared, and figure out how you can stay involved with and assist the communities you've encountered.

Consider the transforming potential of volunteerism and community involvement in promoting global citizenship and good social change. Take this chapter's possibilities, tales, and encounters as a call to action to start your community participation journey and to change the world wherever you go.

Let the values and strategies in this chapter direct you toward life-changing experiences that improve and affect local communities and contribute your time and talents to worthwhile causes globally. This will ensure that you make a lasting legacy of good change.

• Traveler's Resources and Further Reading

With our carefully chosen collection of traveler's resources and recommended reading, you may set off on a voyage of continuous research and discovery that will enrich your travels and motivate your next journeys. With the help of helpful instructions, motivational tales, and knowledgeable insights, we hope you will delve deeper into the world of travel in this chapter and expand your horizons.

1.Overview of Traveler's Resources: Start your investigation with an overview of traveler's resources, a plethora of knowledge, and ideas to help you organize, get ready, and maximize your trip experiences. Find out about the range of resources accessible to travelers, such as online forums, blogs, and social media platforms that provide information, recommendations, and first-hand experiences from experts and other travelers, in addition to guidebooks and travel websites.

2. Useful information and recommendations: Learn useful information and recommendations to help you deal with the challenges of traveling, such as safety tips, transportation hacks, and guidance on packing necessities and budgeting. Look through resources that address a variety of travel-related subjects, such as luxury travel, adventure travel, solo travel, and family travel, to discover the tips and recommendations that most closely match your travel interests and style.

3. Inspirational Tales and Travel Memoirs: Dive into the realm of travel with tales of inspiration and travel memoirs that encapsulate the spirit of discovery and the transforming potential of adventure. Read about incredible travel experiences, cross-cultural interactions, and self-discoveries to satiate your desire and motivate you to go off on your global explorations.

4. Destination Guides and Cultural Insights: Use these resources to learn more about the places you want to visit. They include insider knowledge, background on the area, and useful advice to help you get the most out of your trip. Investigate sites that offer in-depth information on certain areas, towns, and nations to learn more about their distinctive cultures, customs, and tourist attractions.

5. Travel Photography and Art: Using resources that include breathtaking photos and artworks influenced by the marvels of the globe, explore the beauty of travel through the lenses of photography and art. Discover photographic books, coffee table books, and online galleries that, through their vivid pictures and visual narrative, transport you to far-off places and capture the spirit of travel.

6. Guides to Responsible Tourism and Sustainable Travel: Learn more about responsible tourism and sustainable travel by using tools and guides that provide real-world guidance, case studies, and success stories from all around the world. Find more about responsible wildlife tourism, eco-friendly lodging, community-based tourism programs, and ethical volunteer activities that support the economic, social, and

environmental well-being of travel destinations and surrounding communities.

Consider the plethora of reading material and resources at visitors' disposal, as well as the countless chances they present for more exploration and learning. Think of this chapter's tales, tips, and observations as a roadmap for broadening your horizons, organizing your next journey, and getting the most out of your trips.

Let the knowledge and inspiration that you find as you explore the traveler's resources and further reading suggested in this chapter lead you to novel insights, significant encounters, and life-changing events that will enhance your voyage and create a lasting impression on your spirit.

Conclusion

It's time to stop and take stock of the experiences, memories, and lessons we've gained as we near the end of our voyage across California's varied landscapes, fascinating history, and dynamic culture. We hope you will join us in this final chapter as we say goodbye to the Golden State and take the spirit of California with us on our travels. We welcome you to join us in a moment of meditation and thanks.

1. Reflecting on the Journey: From the sun-drenched beaches of Southern California to the towering redwoods of the north, and the vibrant cities, sleepy villages, and breathtaking natural wonders that lie in between, take a minute to reflect on the journey we've taken together. Think back to the sights, sounds, and events that have deeply impacted your spirit, as well as the tales, adventures, and interactions that have expanded your knowledge of our lively and diverse state.

2. Gratitude for the Experience: Thank you for the chance to discover California's treasures and for the honor of being able to personally see its splendor, diversity, and friendliness.
Recognize the contributions made by the individuals, groups, and communities who have embraced us, shared their customs and experiences, and helped to make our journey special and significant.

3. Embracing the Spirit of Adventure: As you go forward, take the spirit of California with you and embrace the spirit of exploration, adventure, and discovery that has driven your journeys through this amazing state. Allow the experiences

and memories you've accumulated in California to motivate you to go on new journeys, make new friends, and welcome the unknown with open arms and hearts.

4. Commitment to Responsible Travel: Stress the value of conserving California's natural and cultural legacy for future generations to enjoy. Reiterate your commitment to sustainable tourism practices and responsible travel. Commit to travel with awareness, to protect the environment, to help the people you visit, and to make decisions that will have the least negative impact possible.

5. Continuing the trip: Remember that this is just the beginning of our trip as we say goodbye to California. Take with you the knowledge, insights, and adventures from our time together as you venture out into the world and uncover new frontiers. Keep in mind that whenever you're ready to come back and have new experiences, California will always be here, ready to embrace you with open arms.

6. Goodbye and Bon Voyage: With a spirit of adventure and a heart full of appreciation, we bid California farewell and turn our attention to other adventures and places that lie ahead.
I hope your next travels are full of wonder, learning, and the excitement of adventure. Bon voyage, dear traveler. We would like to take this opportunity to express our sincere gratitude to you, our fellow traveler, for accompanying us on this incredible adventure as we complete the last chapter of our travel guide to California. I hope that the events and memories we have shared will motivate you to keep discovering,

developing, and learning as you make your way through the amazing fabric of our planet.

Printed in Great Britain
by Amazon